CALGARY

HEART OF THE NEW WEST

URBAN
TAPESTRY
SERIES

TOWERY
PUBLISHING, INC.

CALGARY

HEART OF THE NEW WEST

INTRODUCTION BY

DARREL JANZ

ART DIRECTION BY

KAREN GEARY

SPONSORED BY

**PROMOTING
CALGARY, INC.**

Contents

Delta Hotels

TELUS

TELUS

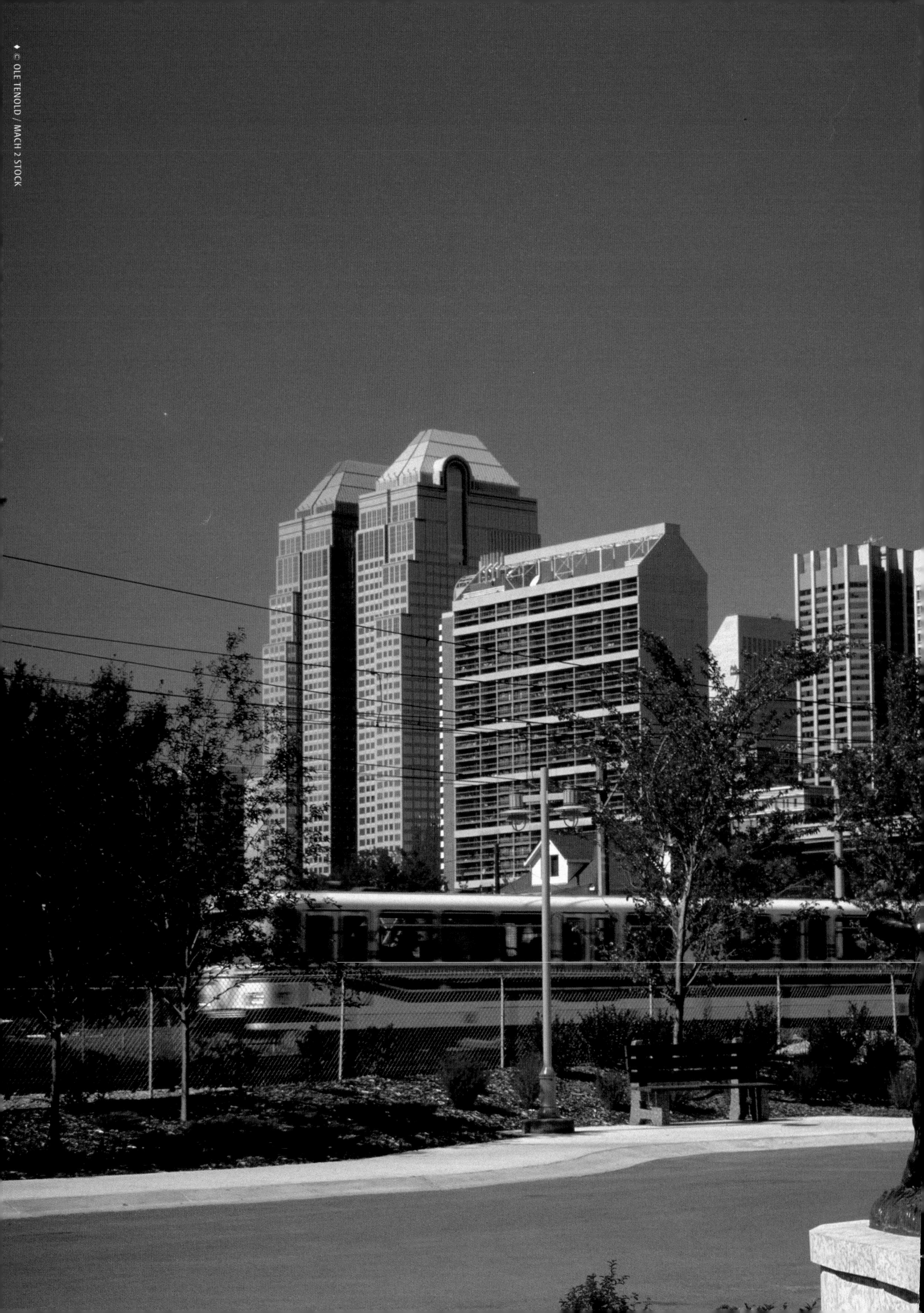

© OLE TENOLD / MACH 2 STOCK

CALGARY

by
Darrel Janz

I t is a great honour for me to have been asked to write the introduction to this fine pictorial book about my adopted city. The majority of us who live and work in this jewel of the Alberta foothills have adopted Calgary. Or maybe it would be more appropriate to say it has adopted us. Some of us came from other parts of Canada; others came from next door in the United States, while still others have arrived from places literally all over the world. Many came thinking their stay would be relatively brief. I came in 1973, intending to stay for about five years. But for most of us, something happened. This beautiful city took us in and, somewhere along the way, leaving became unthinkable.

When I arrived, the population was around 400,000, and I sensed that Calgary and Calgarians were struggling with the city's identity. Was it to remain the world's best-known Cowtown, or was it to grow into something else?

It has been a pleasure to watch Calgary grow into the thriving business centre it is today, second only to Toronto among Canadian cities in numbers of corporate head offices. It has been a delight to see it develop a reputation for its arts and cultural community, all the while maintaining its reputation as, yes, the world's best-known Cowtown.

Even with a population rapidly approaching a million, Calgary has also remained the friendliest, most caring city anyone could hope to live and work in. It's an honour not only to have watched it grow, but also to have been very much involved in that growth. ▶

I grew up on a farm/ranch in southwestern Saskatchewan. As a boy, one of my dreams was to compete at the Calgary Stampede, known for good reason as The Greatest Outdoor Show on Earth. It wasn't a realistic dream, because I wasn't a very good cowboy. When my brothers and some friends and I would ride steers, I seldom managed to stay on for the mandatory eight seconds. However, that didn't stop me from dreaming of becoming a champion bull rider and a driver in the world famous Rangeland Derby, the chuckwagon races that are a large part of what makes the Stampede so much more than just another big rodeo. My only experience at the reins was driving to school in a buggy pulled by our old black mare and occasionally handling a two-horse team pulling a hay wagon. Every evening during the Stampede, I'd tune in to CFCN Radio and listen to the late Henry Viney broadcast the chuckwagon races. In the 1950s, there weren't as many radio stations as there are now, so the signal from CFCN came through loud and clear despite the distance of more than 400 kilometres. Even now I can hear Henry's distinctive voice yell: "There's the claxon and there they GOOOOO!" When the races were over, I'd go back outside and dream of driving against names like Glass, Willard, Cosgrave, and Dorchester.

Little did I dream that the Stampede would become a big part of my life, not as a competitor but as one who covers this great annual event for Calgary, Southern Alberta, and occasionally for all of Canada.

Even more remote was the probability that I would be in the Eye in the Sky, as the Stampede press box is known, with Henry when he did his final chuckwagon broadcast in the mid-1970s. By then I was employed by CFCN Television, the little sister of CFCN Radio. Today, the radio station bears different call letters and the television operation is a highly successful part of the Canadian Television Network (CTV). ▶

12

Not only the Stampede, but all of Calgary, has become a big part of my life. And I'm deeply humbled and honoured to have been a part of Calgary's life in the last quarter of the 20th century and the first part of the new millennium. Since 1973, I have had the great pleasure of being able to tell this wonderful, thriving city about itself and its people each evening at six o' clock.

hen I arrived here after honing my journalistic skills in Montréal and London, Ontario, it was like coming home. As much as I'd enjoyed my time in eastern Canada, Calgary felt so comfortable. Our city hall reporter and weekend anchor at CFCN in my early years was a young man named Ralph Klein (below, on right). His experience covering city hall convinced Ralph that the city could be run better than it was. So, he became a candidate for mayor in 1980, running against an incumbent who seemed a pretty good bet for re-election—the late Ross Alger. We who had worked with Ralph expected him to do okay, but we didn't think he'd win. We thought he'd get it out of his system and come back to work with us.

Well, we underestimated our cohort. Since 1973, there have been many provincial elections in Alberta and even more civic elections in Calgary. I've covered them all, and the only exciting one was the 1980 mayoralty election, when this dark horse from our newsroom beat the odds and won.

After eight years as mayor, Ralph decided to move up to provincial politics. By now no one was betting against him and, in 1989, he was elected to the Legislative Assembly of Alberta and became a minister in the cabinet of Premier Don Getty. When Getty decided to retire in the early nineties, it came as no surprise when Ralph announced that he would seek the leadership of the Progressive Conservative party. His winning streak remained intact and, since 1993, I've been calling the guy who used to be my backup Mr. Premier. ▶

© DAVE OLECKO

Going back to that 1980 civic election, it was the only exciting one because all the others, both provincial and civic, have been incredibly one-sided. Allan Blakeney, a former premier of Saskatchewan, once said that Albertans don't elect governments—they elect dynasties. The same could be said for Calgarians. After his initial close win, Ralph won the next two elections with around 90 percent of the popular vote. His successor, Al Duerr, has continued that tradition. On the provincial political scene, the story has been the same.

In fact, since 1971, when native Calgarian Peter Lougheed began a 14-year tenure as Premier of Alberta, the tradition of the political dynasty has been solid. If you study Alberta history, you'll see that the only close elections are the ones where there's a change in governing parties. It seems Albertans like to elect people they trust, and then get on with their own business while the politicians look after the affairs of the province or city, whichever the case may be. For his part, Lougheed served the province with great distinction and led it through a period of incredible growth. Since retiring from elected office, he has gone on to become a senior statesman on the Canadian political scene.

Speaking of government, many early Calgarians felt their city, rather than Edmonton, should be the provincial capital. At first some felt slighted that the honour went to our neighbor to the north. But they didn't stew about it for long. Instead, they set out to make Calgary the business capital of Alberta.

Ours is a young city. One of its oldest buildings is a little clapboard structure that served as the office of Peter Prince, one of the area's pioneer entrepreneurs. That building is now a breakfast restaurant, known as the 1886 Buffalo Café, so named because 1886 was the year that Prince incorporated the Eau Claire & Bow River Lumber Company, which he ran from that building. It's one of the most popular breakfast spots in the downtown area, and it's said that a lot of deals are begun or consummated there over an early morning omelette. ▶

© AL CHAREST

C A L G A R Y

The restaurant gained international fame during the 1988 Winter Olympics, when it was featured in a commercial that ran frequently on the ABC Television Network during its Olympic coverage. The following summer, the father of some friends of mine came to visit from California and said he'd like to go for breakfast at "that 1886 place" he'd seen on television during the Olympics.

The little white building with the black shingled roof sits nestled among the modern structures in the Eau Claire Market area. The sign over the front door still says "Eau Claire & Bow River Lumber Co." Prince came here from Eau Claire, Wisconsin, in the late 1800s; hence, the area near the Bow River became known as Eau Claire. It's doubly suitable because *eau claire* in French means "clear water," and except for spring runoff time, the water in the Bow is crystal clear. A beautiful island park in the river bears Peter Prince's name, serving as a lasting memorial to a man who set an example for succeeding generations of Calgarians to follow.

The basement of the building is a little museum of early Calgary. There are numerous artifacts from Prince's lumber and coal business and a wonderful gallery of photographs of the dangerous springtime log runs from the eastern slopes of the Rocky Mountains, down the swift-flowing Kananaskis and Bow rivers to his sawmill in town. Calgary wasn't a city yet. Prince also brought hydro-electric power to Calgary by harnessing the waters of the rivers and running lines to the town.

In addition, there are photos of early Calgary and some of its pioneer residents. You'll see numerous shots of the Prince and Lougheed families. Our former

premier's grandfather, Sir James Lougheed, was a prominent early Calgarian who came from eastern Canada to establish a law practice.

Prince, Lougheed, and many others came here in the late 1800s, with a vision and, no doubt, with a real sense of adventure. This was, after all, the frontier. Not many years before they came, the Northwest Mounted Police, under the command of Colonel James MacLeod, had established a fort at the confluence of the Bow and Elbow rivers. The Mounties were here to ensure the safe and peaceful settlement of the area. Part of that original fort has been restored, and it has become a popular tourist attraction, as well as a fine educational resource to help teach the younger generation and newcomers about their city's beginnings. On our long summer evenings, the shadows of modern sky-scrapers creep over the old fort as the sun sets in the northwest.

I can only imagine what those pioneers thought when they first laid eyes on the majestic Rocky Mountains and the beautiful, gently rolling foothills, seeming almost to bow before them.

I remember my reaction the first time I came to the city in the early 1960s. The view, as I approached from the east, took my breath away. It was early spring, and the mountains were still covered with snow, while the foothills were bare, waiting for the first green grass and wildflowers to appear.

Now, whenever I leave this area, the greatest thrill on my return is that first glimpse of the Rockies as I approach from the east. I can no longer imagine living any place where I couldn't see them and ski them. ▶

People used to complain that the only good restaurants in Calgary were steak houses. But today, thanks at least in part to many of these new Canadians, the dining choices are much more varied. I need to emphasize, though, that Alberta beef remains a highly popular choice when locals and visitors go for dinner here.

Another result of this ethnic influx is that Calgary has become well-known for its cultural diversity. If someone visited the city only at Stampede time, they might get the impression that the only music played here is country and western. True, we have produced many fine country performers and are home to the Canadian Country Music Hall of Fame. However, the music base here is much broader than that. The Calgary Philharmonic is widely regarded as one of the finest orchestras in the country. In recent years, it has attracted top musical directors, like Mario Bernardi and Hans Graf. The Philharmonic stages a variety of events to expose itself to the community at large and rid itself of the elitist aura that often surrounds classical music. Events like Mozart on the Mountain and Beethoven on the Bow have been huge successes. Calgary's opera company has also gained an enviable reputation, and all its productions are virtual sell-outs. There are also two fine professional theatre companies, as well as numerous smaller semiprofessional and amateur groups. ▶

Still, our biggest cultural event by far remains the Stampede. For 10 days each July, this increasingly cosmopolitan city returns to its Cowtown roots and throws a good old-fashioned western party for the world.

Suits and ties are hung in the closet—or sent to the dry cleaners—while western wear becomes standard attire. Go into corporate boardrooms during Stampede, and you'll see blue jeans, big belt buckles, and fancy western-style shirts—maybe even cowboy hats on the table, or on the heads of those around the table. When a Calgarian sees someone downtown in a business suit at Stampede time, a common comment is: "Must be from Toronto or Vancouver."

Speaking of boardrooms, when people think of Calgary in a business sense, they think oil and natural gas—understandably so, because that remains a big part of what corporate Calgary is and does. However, the petroleum industry has been instrumental in attracting a much broader range of businesses to the city. Now, we're also becoming known as a leader in the high-tech field.

When a city does business with the world, it needs a world-class airport, and Calgary has that. The Calgary Airport Authority has turned the airport into a showpiece that amazes travelers from all over the globe. Not only is it attractive, but many people who do a great deal of flying tell me it's also wonderfully efficient.

Another of Calgary's big industries is education. In fact, the city boasts the best-educated populace in Canada. There are two fine publicly funded school systems, numerous private and parochial schools, and a variety of post-secondary institutes. The University of Calgary (U of C), Mount Royal College, and the Southern Alberta Institute of Technology are world-class schools of higher learning. Each offers a broad range of educational opportunities, but each has also carved a niche for itself in specific areas.

▲ © PETER SAUNDERS / MACH 2 STOCK

The U of C is the newest of the three, having gained autonomy from the University of Alberta in Edmonton in 1966. Since then, it has grown to become one of the most innovative and research-intensive universities in Canada. Its research covers such diverse areas as medicine, law, the family, energy, the environment, the Arctic, and computer software.

The oldest post-secondary institute in Calgary, and one of the oldest in Alberta, is Mount Royal College. Its first campus opened downtown in 1910, under the sponsorship of the Methodist Church. Today the college sits on a former Royal Canadian Air Force base in southwest Calgary. It offers a wide range of degree and diploma programs, and its graduates are in great demand in such areas as nursing, journalism, public relations, broadcasting, and criminology.

The Southern Alberta Institute of Technology, known as SAIT, has had a reputation for providing quality technical education, going all the way back to 1916. SAIT's mission is to meet the practical needs of its students and their prospective employers. Today it trains people in such diverse fields as automotive, television, radio, dental, and computer technologies.

The reputations of all three institutions have spread far beyond Canada's borders, and today many international students are enrolled.

The world has learned much about our city through such international events as the 1988 Winter Olympics, the 1997 World Police and Fire Games, and the 2000 World Petroleum Congress. One of the things people involved in those events found most impressive was the incredible volunteer spirit in Calgary. When the call goes out for volunteers, Calgarians respond in a way unmatched elsewhere. ▶

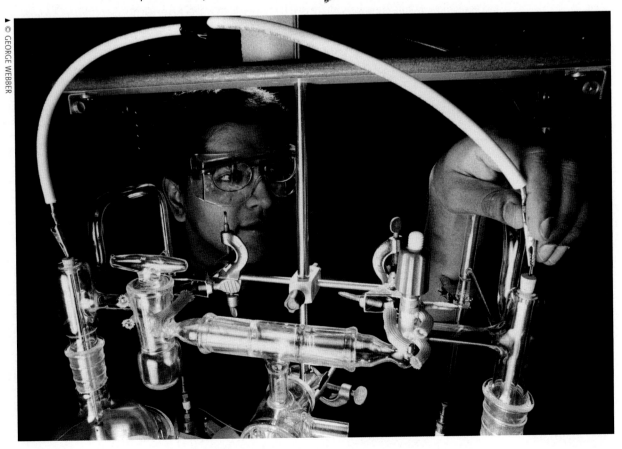

© GEORGE WEBBER

Our city's big heart is evidenced by the fact that since the mid-1980s, the United Way campaign has exceeded its goal each year. And that spirit starts at an early age. When a British program called Operation Christmas Child (OCC) was brought to North America in the early 1990s by the relief agency Samaritan's Purse, Calgary schools quickly became the biggest contributors on the continent. OCC encourages kids in participating countries to pack shoe boxes with gifts for youngsters in the poorest regions of the world.

We in Calgary are blessed with wonderful recreational facilities and great sports entertainment. The most obvious of these are the National Hockey League Flames, the Canadian Football League Stampeders, and the Pacific Coast Baseball League Cannons. But, there's also great junior hockey and some of the best university and college athletics in the country. The facilities built for the Olympics ensure we have annual World Cup bobsled, luge, and speed skating events. Many speed skaters say the ice in our Olympic Oval is the best in the world. In recent years, more records have been broken here than on any other track.

For those who'd rather do than watch, we have something for everyone. There's a great path system for biking, jogging, and in-line skating. We have dozens of indoor arenas where those who can't get enough hockey can play year-round. Soccer and rugby have become extremely popular with young Calgarians in recent years, and there are great facilities for these sports. Thousands of people of all ages continue to play baseball and softball. We also enjoy a great variety of golf courses, from challenging championship links to the kind where even a duffer like me can keep his score respectable.

There is so much more I could say about this wonderful city. I could talk about its great health care system and the wonderful facilities for the elderly. I could talk about how visitors are always impressed by how safe they feel here, even when they go out for an evening stroll in the downtown area. Our police force is highly regarded across North America and in many other parts of the world.

I feel privileged to call Calgary home and to have this opportunity to write about it. Now it's time to let the camera take over and show you the city's beauty and its uniqueness. ❧

ALTHOUGH SITUATED AT THE WESTERN end of more than 1,600 kilometres of prairie, Calgary is hardly out of touch. The Trans-Canada Highway passes through the city, and easy access to and from the United States ensures a steady flow of vehicles transporting residents and visitors alike.

CALGARY'S BEAUTIFUL BUILDINGS reflect a melding of form and function. Amid the city's architectural splendor, the world's largest elevated-walkway system (BOTTOM)—known locally as the +15, a reference to its location 15 feet above street level—allows pedestrians to pass between buildings without subjecting themselves to the vagaries of weather or traffic.

▼ © VIC TUCKER / MACH 2 STOCK

AFTER 12 YEARS OF LEADING CALGARY through an unprecedented period of expansion, Al Duerr voluntarily hung up his mayoral hat in October 2001 (PAGES 30-33). During his four terms in office, the enormously popular politico held fast to an agenda that attempted to balance economic growth with community resources.

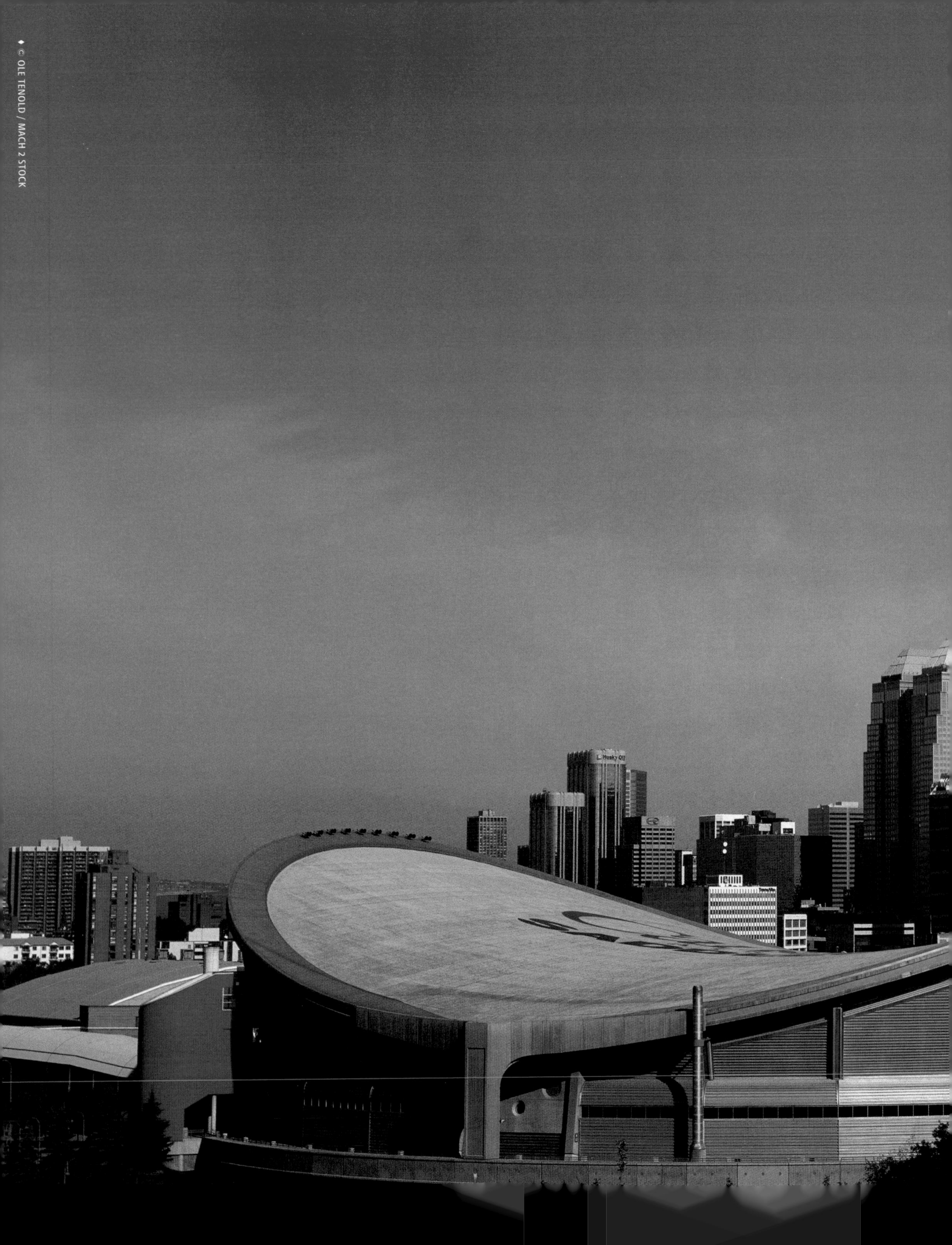

© OLE TENOLD / MACH 2 STOCK

VIEWED FROM A DISTANCE, CALGARY'S sleek skyline features such easily identifiable landmarks as the Saddle Dome and the Calgary Tower. Upon closer inspection, the downtown area's looming edifices paint a vivid contrast between old and new (PAGES 36 AND 37).

THE CALGARY REGION BOASTS A RICH aeronautic history (PAGES 38-41). At the Aero Space Museum (OPPOSITE), the collection includes vintage aircraft from World Wars I and II, as well as civil aviation and recreational planes. Some 40 kilometres outside the city, the town of High River uses one of its many outdoor murals (ABOVE) to commemorate the flight school established by the British Commonwealth Air Training Plan during World War II.

CALGARY

SPENDING A NIGHT IN AN AUTHENTIC teepee—not to be confused with an artistic facsimile on the University of Calgary campus (OPPOSITE)—helps visitors to Head-Smashed-in Buffalo Jump experience life during the heyday of the Blackfoot. Once the proud occupants of territory ranging from the North Saskatchewan River in Alberta to Montana's Yellowstone River, the tribe is honored today at a $10 million interpretive centre, located approximately 180 kilometres southwest of Calgary.

AS THE OWNER OF ALL IT SURVEYS, A feathered friend pauses to contemplate the city from a vantage point above Calgary's Olympic Plaza. A painted counterpart takes flight in artist Doug Driediger's *Giving Wings to the Dream,* a 409-square-metre mural on the Calgary Urban Project Society building.

N FRONT OF OLYMPIC PLAZA'S TEATRO, a maquette of Barbara Paterson's *Women are Persons!* bears mute testimony to the strides made in women's rights during the last century. The piece pays tribute to the Famous Five—Henrietta Muir Edwards, Nellie McClung, Louise McKinney, Emily Murphy, and Irene Parlby—who lobbied in the 1920s for the right of women to serve as senators. A larger-than-life version of the sculpture was installed on Parliament Hill in 2000.

CALGARY

ART AND LIFE FACE OFF IN VARIOUS SPOTS around Calgary's Century Gardens. Inside the downtown public space, J. Seward Johnson Jr.'s *The Winner* (OPPOSITE) provides a challenge for any future chess champion. Outside, pedestrian talk meets its match in William Mcelchern's *Conversation* (ABOVE).

52

THERE'S GOT TO BE AN EASIER WAY to make a living: cheered on by an enraptured audience, professional riders compete to lasso millions of dollars in Calgary Stampede prize money.

THE YEAR 1998 MARKED THE 75TH anniversary of the Calgary Stampede's Chuckwagon Racing. Although thousands vie for seats from which to watch the races, some fans prefer a quieter vantage point. Others reap the benefits of the chuckwagon's more traditional role by heeding the call of the dinner bell.

THE CALM BEFORE THE STORM: EXPERTS at their craft, professional cowboys at the Calgary Stampede prepare for a little bronco busting—with the knowledge that they'll soon be hanging on for dear life.

© BRIAN STABLYK

© FRANK JOHNSON / MACH 2 STOCK

CLOWNING AROUND ISN'T ALL IT'S cracked up to be. Injuries during a rodeo are well-nigh inevitable, but often the greatest dangers threaten the rodeo clowns, who consistently risk their lives to divert angry bulls from fallen riders.

© BILL MARSH / MACH 2 STOCK

A WOMAN'S PLACE IS IN THE RODEO: barrel racing may be the best-known women's event at the Calgary Stampede, but participating cowgirls are free to compete in other ways as well, including the Calgary Stampede Queen contest (PAGES 65-67). Reigning royals (OPPOSITE) from other area rodeos attend the Stampede each year as honoured guests.

COMBINING DISCIPLINE WITH ENTERTAIN-
ment, the Royal Canadian Mounted
Police Musical Ride traces its roots back
more than a century. The basic formations of the Musical Ride evolved from those of
cavalry drills, and members of the Ride tour
the country each year, delighting audiences
of all ages.

CALGARY

PROFESSIONAL RODEO COWBOYS Association World Champion All Around Cowboy Fred Whitfield (ABOVE) ropes in the crowds at the Stampede as he demonstrates his world-renowned lassoing skills. Native American performers generate an equal amount of audience interest with their breathtaking displays of traditional hoop dances (OPPOSITE).

NATIVE AMERICANS TRAVEL FROM all parts of Alberta to honor ancient customs at the Stampede. Former rodeo star John Scott (OPPOSITE) makes his living these days with the Longview-based John Scott Motion Picture Animals, Equipment Rentals, which trains a wide range of movie talent from stuntmen and wranglers to birds and monkeys.

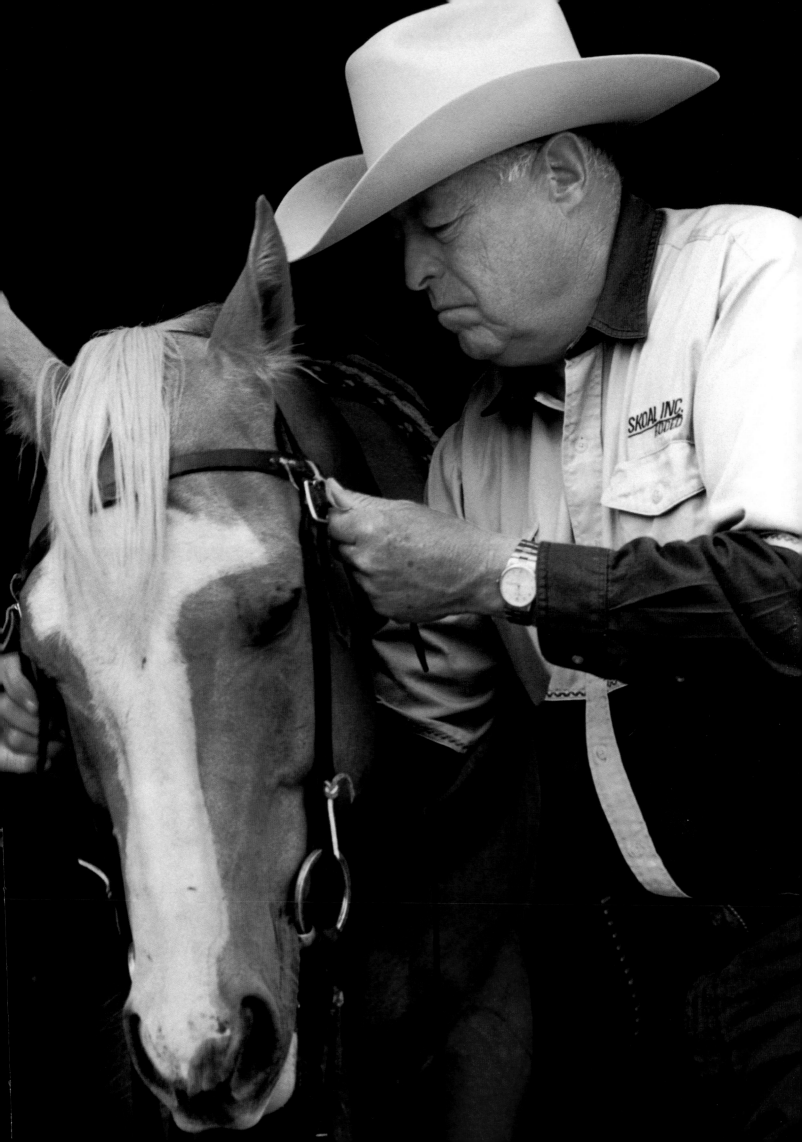

CALGARY

FAR FROM THE MADDING CROWD: Alberta's natural beauty provides plenty to roar about, as residents and visitors alike have discovered. *Grizzly Falls*, filmed in the Kananaskis area—about an hour's drive from Calgary—displays the countryside's mountainous terrain to its best advantage (OPPOSITE).

A WELL-KNOWN FIGURE TO LOCAL music lovers, Calgary Opera's official spokes-puppet, Gertie (ABOVE), demonstrates her civic pride. But it's a display of fangs that makes the point for the creations of actor, writer, and puppeteer Ronnie Burkett. Burkett, whose work has garnered numerous awards, pulls every satirical string to have his Theatre of Marionettes (OPPOSITE) address such heady themes as the artist's place in society.

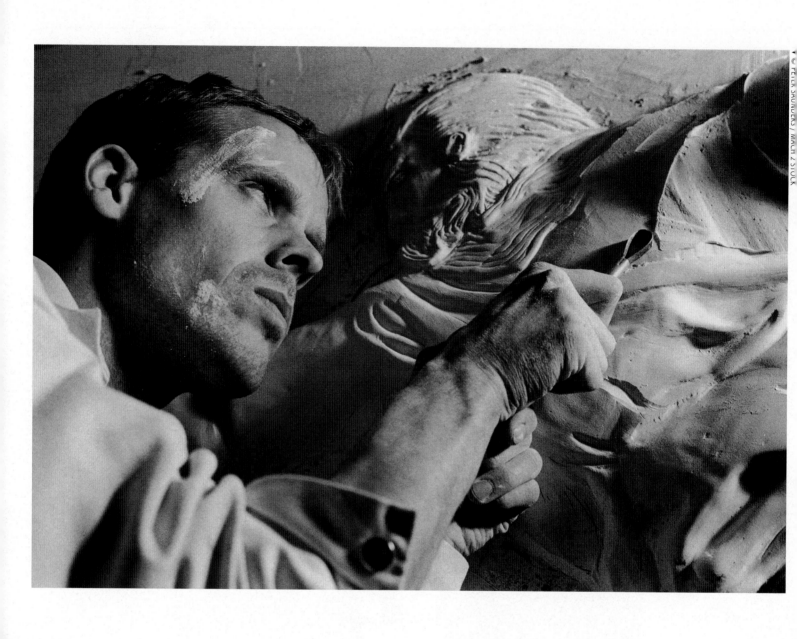

SCULPTORS ILLYAS PAGONIS AND ADRIAN Robberstad (ABOVE) did their part to make Calgary a better place when they restored one of the stone lions that guarded the Centre Street Bridge—then made a mould of the original and recast four replacement cats. Lending a unique look to some of the city's interiors, Calgary-based artist Trevor Duvall (OPPOSITE) sculpts three-dimensional works of art into the walls and ceilings of prestigious area houses.

F ROM EVENTS AT THE CHINESE CULTURAL Centre to fancy footwork on stage, the city's rich arts scene is growing by leaps and bounds. The Alberta Ballet, the fourth-largest dance company in Canada, performs September through April each year, and features the talents of dancers like Tanya Dobler (LEFT).

UNDER THE TUTELAGE OF NOTED Musical Director Hans Graf (OPPOSITE), the Calgary Philharmonic Orchestra, formed in 1955, offers performances including annual classical, baroque, and pops series. In 2000, the orchestra completed its first tour of Europe, giving highly successful performances at 12 cities in Austria, Germany, Switzerland, and France during a two-week period.

MUSIC IS ALWAYS IN THE AIR IN Calgary—at least in its streets. From percussionists in marching bands to bagpipers at the annual Calgary Highland Games (RIGHT), local musicians have the brass it takes to strut their musical stuff.

CANADIAN COUNTRY MUSIC STARS aren't a new breed, but the current generation of singer/songwriters is sweeping the world off its feet. Albertan Terri Clark (ABOVE) carries on her family's country-music legacy, reaping awards from all quarters, while internationally acclaimed Shania Twain (RIGHT) continues to charm Calgary with her captivating performances. Native Calgarian Paul Brandt (OPPOSITE TOP) has won multiple awards since releasing his first album in 1996. In fact, local music is so good, it's got people dancing in the streets (PAGES 94 AND 95).

HEART OF THE NEW WEST

96

MEN OF VISION: AT HIS RANCH NORTH of Cochrane, self-taught painter and sculptor Mac MacKenzie (ABOVE) houses his own foundry and gallery. His more than 100 bronze sculptures are depictions of cowboy and wildlife themes that resonate with Alberta's ranching history. Transplanted San Franciscan David Wilkie earned the nickname The Mandolin Kid—also the title of his first solo album— for his hauntingly beautiful music. Both musician and composer, he has recorded with such notables as Maria Muldaur and Oscar Lopez.

T DOESN'T MATTER HOW OLD YOU are, what sort of skiing you prefer, or whether you ski competitively or just for fun: the Alberta Rockies, from Banff and Jasper to Canada Olympic Park, are a skier's paradise (PAGES 100-105).

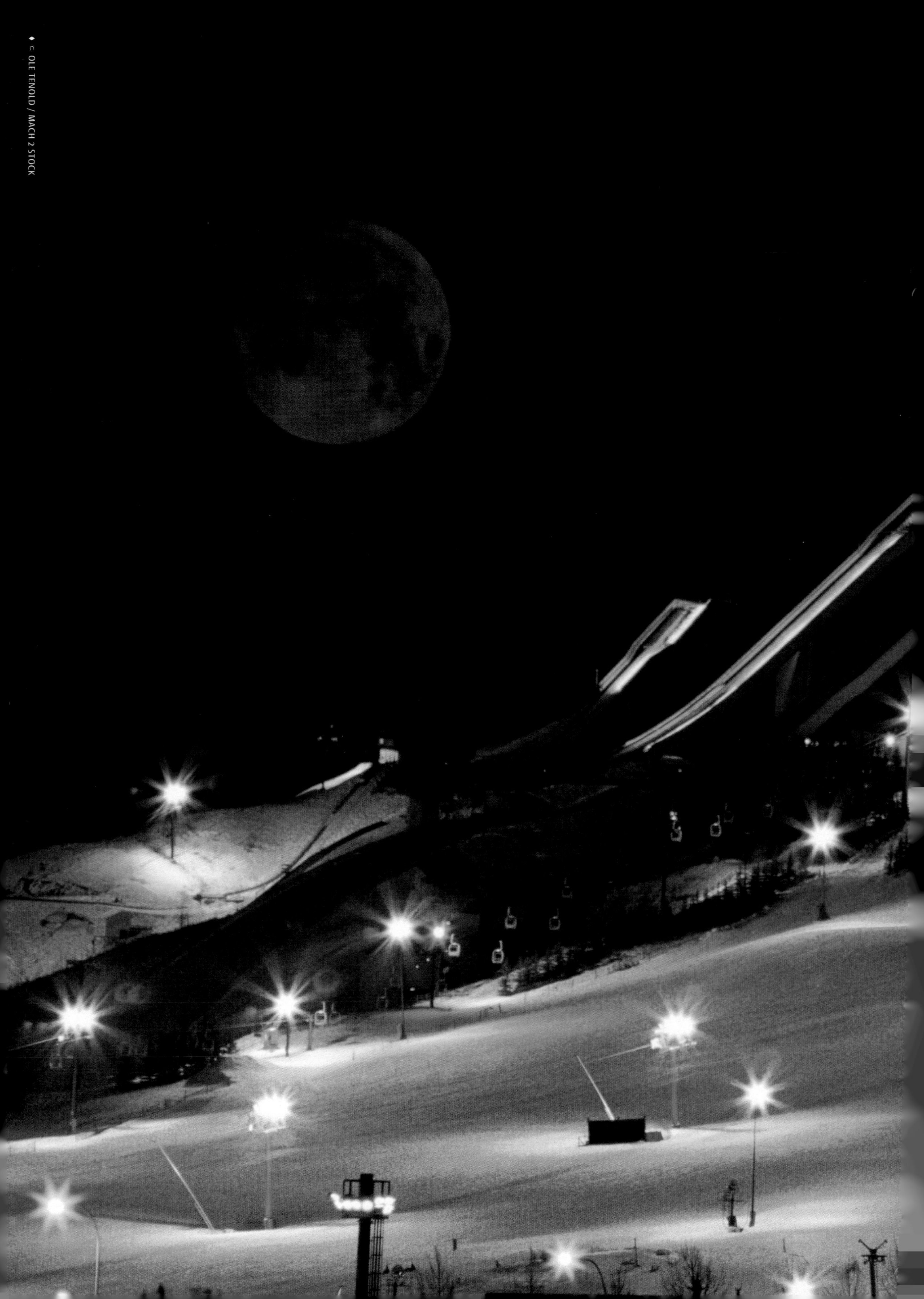

© OLE TENOLD / MACH 2 STOCK

ALTHOUGH SOME CALGARIANS THINK they receive more than enough snow during the long winter months, snowboarding enthusiasts know better. Those who can't get enough of this extreme sport during the traditional 'boarding season now have the opportunity to participate in or watch the Molson Canadian Rocks DV8 Urban Street Festival (OPPOSITE) each July. Some 100,000 kilograms of snow were trucked into downtown Calgary for the 2000 festival, which attracted more than 40,000 attendees.

14

12

10

8

6

4

2

MUSHERS, GET A MOVE ON: SINCE 1983, the Alberta International Sled Dog Classic has been held in Canmore, just short of an hour's drive from Calgary. The event features more than 100 teams competing for cash prizes in sled racing and skijoring.

C A L G A R Y

WATER, WATER EVERYWHERE: AS THE winter snow melts in the Alberta Rockies, those casting about for something to do may elect to make a splash—with or without the aid of rod, reel, or boat (PAGES 113-121).

CALGARY

122

SWIMMERS JOANNE MALAR AND CURTIS Myden (OPPOSITE) aren't just a flash in the pan when it comes to striking pure gold—or silver or bronze—leaving young Canadian swimmers with no shortage of role models at whom to goggle. Calgarian Myden's medals include a bronze from the 2000 Olympic Games and two silvers from the 1999 Pan Pacific Championships. Malar, a native of Hamilton, Ontario, has earned more than two dozen national championships, and she took home three gold medals from the 1999 Pan-American Games.

THOSE MORE FAMILIAR WITH WATER traps than with pools, lakes, or rivers may bring golf to the fore of their recreational plans. Calgary and the surrounding area boast more than a score of golf courses and driving ranges. Other Calgarians get their sports needs met in more physical pursuits (PAGES 126 AND 127).

IRING OFF ONE HIT AFTER ANOTHER, THE Calgary Cannons—with the help of their popular mascot, Wabash—have packed the stands at Burns Stadium every season since 1985. The Cannons are the Triple-A Pacific Coast League affiliate of the Florida Marlins.

T h

t

c

Hitm

© IAN TOMLINSON / ALLSPORT

ANNING THE FIRE OF THE CITY'S HOCKEY fever, the Calgary Flames do their best to put opponents on ice. Off the rink, the Flames Foundation has sparked more than $17 million in donations to southern Alberta charities since 1980.

© ELSA / ALLSPORT

CALGARY

WHATEVER SKILL AN EVENT CALLS for, Calgary's athletes don't steer away from the one-on-one matches that make local sports so exciting.

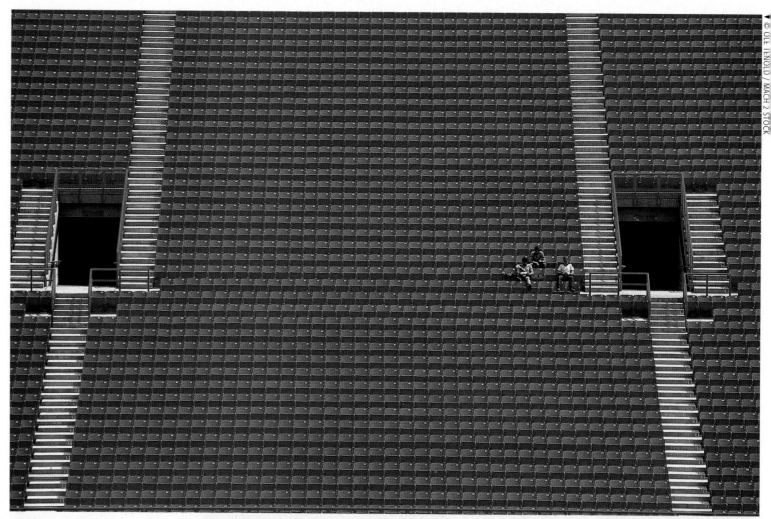

McMahon Stadium, opened in 1960, rolls out the red carpet for fans of the Canadian Football League's Calgary Stampeders and the team's cheerleaders, the Outriders. Since their first season, the Stampeders have played in nine CFL Grey Cup Championships, winning a quartet of the coveted cups.

C A L G A R Y

137

© JOHN WHISSON / MACH 2 STOCK

© HELGA PATTISON-DAUER / MACH 2 STOCK

© BILL MARSH / MACH 2 STOCK

138

CALGARY

FF TO THE RACES: THE FLEET OF FOOT, hoof, or wheel have numerous opportunities to compete in contests in and around Calgary.

HARNESSING HORSEPOWER IS A BREEZE for some Calgarians, whose alternative modes of transportation allow them to move like the wind—whether they're heading to work, or just revving around town.

SURROUNDED BY THE LUSH MAJESTY of the Alberta Rockies, the Fairmont Banff Springs Hotel is eminently suited to its location. This landmark hotel—modelled in the style of a 19th-century Scottish castle—originally opened in 1888. Although the area's primary attractions at that time were the nearby hot springs, the hotel today offers guests an abundance of recreational options, including white-water rafting in the summer and canyon ice walks during the winter season.

THE RESORT TOWN OF BANFF (OPPOSITE) is a 130-kilometre, scenic drive from Calgary along the Trans-Canada Highway. Banff's stunning location, in the heart of Banff National Park and overlooking the Bow River, makes the area a year-round travel destination for curious creatures of every kind.

TAKE A WALK ON ALBERTA'S WILD SIDE BY embarking on a nature hike, an airplane adventure, or a motorbus tour. The region's natural beauty serves as a haven for startling menageries of wildlife, whether visitors opt to view them from the land, air, or water.

LIKE ITS NEIGHBOR BANFF, LAKE LOUISE owes much of its early popularity to the construction of Canada's first transcontinental railroad. Today, the Fairmont Chateau Lake Louise (PAGES 148-150) extends its hospitality to visitors year-round. The wintry, turquoise lake itself springs from Victoria Glacier.

ALBERTA'S CANOLA FIELDS ARE BEAUTIFUL when viewed during their midsummer flowering, but the annual harvest is worth its weight in gold. Each year, the province exports some $400 million in canola—to be used in products including cattle feed, oil, and margarine.

TO MARKET, TO MARKET: AGRICULTURE is the primary means of livelihood for most Hutterite colonies. This Anabaptist-sect offshoot, named for early leader Jacob Hutter, has lived communally and simply since the mid-16th century. Today, Hutterite colonies can be found scattered across western Canada and the northern United States.

LBERTA'S FINAL FRONTIER MAY BE THE town of Vulcan (THIS PAGE), approximately 120 kilometres southeast of Calgary. Since the early 1990s, this enterprising farming community has bolstered its fragile economy by opening all hailing frequencies to tourists—particularly *Star Trek* fans, who beam in in droves for the annual Vul-Con convention.

ALTHOUGH PEOPLE IN SOME AREAS near Calgary may have their heads in the clouds, others remain strictly earthbound. Working ranches thrive as an integral part of this region.

DIMM'S
RANCH

CALGARY

ALGARY MAY HAVE SHED MUCH OF its Cowtown image, but cowboys themselves are far from old hat. Bill Collins (BOTTOM), a former calf-roping and cutting-horse champion, still lives at a gallop, providing expertise and advice for the Calgary Stampede's cutting-horse event.

YA-HA-TINDA—WHICH, TRANSLATED FROM the language of the Stoney Indians, means "plains in the mountains"— stretches for 16 kilometres along the north bank of the Red Deer River. This federal Crown Land is part horse reserve, part wilderness hike, and wholly evocative of the region's living past.

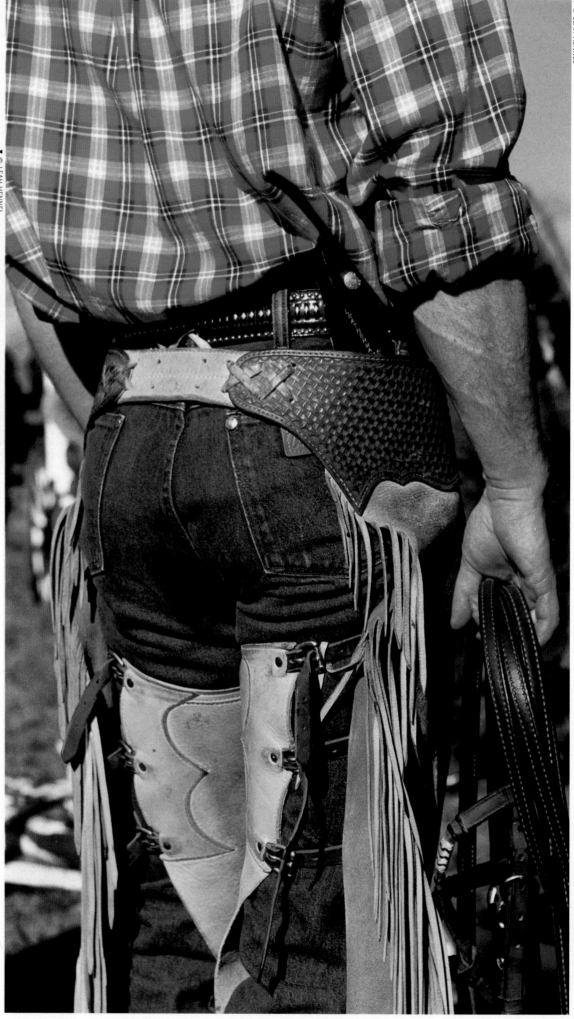

YA HA TINDA

STALLION IN YARD

F OR THOSE WHO DIG DINOSAURS, THE ROYAL Tyrrell Museum of Paleontology (TOP AND OPPOSITE TOP) in Drumheller—about two hours northeast of Calgary—provides a skeleton key to ancient history. The first *Albertosaurus* remains were discovered in the area in 1884, and paleontologists today (BOTTOM) continue to unearth dinosaur bones and other fossils throughout the Drumheller Badlands, which include Horse-shoe Canyon (PAGES 170 AND 171), the first glimpse many have of the badlands.

RELEASE YOUR INNER POLAR BEAR AT THE Calgary Zoo. The zoo, whose residents include owls, tigers, and giraffes, also houses Prehistoric Park, which features life-size models of dinosaurs and information about dinosaur habitats.

CALGARY

THE CALGARY ZOO'S MOST NOTABLE feature may be its conservation program, which provides a refuge for whooping cranes (OPPOSITE) and several other endangered species. In addition, the zoo's Botanical Gardens—one of the largest outdoor gardens in Western Canada—thrives under the stewardship of employees like Master Horticulturist Tian Dalgleish (ABOVE). On a smaller scale, family fun blossoms at northwest Calgary's Riley Park (PAGES 180 AND 181). The park offers gardens, a wading pool, and the opportunity to watch or play cricket on the weekends.

PERHAPS IT'S FASTER TO SHIP A HORSE to the finish line via FedEx than it is to let it run. Either way, it's a fair bet that the dozen people who attended Spruce Meadows' first tournament in 1976 never dreamed that this Calgary venue would one day attract more than 300,000 fans of show-jumping to the National, Canada One, North American, and Masters tournaments each year.

CALGARY'S HERITAGE PARK, THE LARGEST living historical village in Canada, recreates pre-1914 western Canadian life (PAGES 184-187) with restored buildings and interpreters. This non-profit society uses such interactive activities as a steam locomotive, an antique midway, and horse-drawn wagon rides to entertain and amuse.

HISTORICAL RELICS OF CANADA'S OIL and gas past share a place with the region's contemporary exploration efforts. Although Shell Canada didn't move its corporate headquarters to Calgary until 1984, the Shell name has gassed up the country since 1911, when Royal Dutch/Shell Group incorporated in Canada.

HARD TO STEER: MANY OF THE CITY'S residents are tireless when it comes to making a statement, even one as simple as the desire to find their cars easily in parking lots.

O N THE ROAD AGAIN: WITH CALGARY'S thousands of paved roads, more than 5 million metres of sidewalks, nearly 70,000 streetlights, and in excess of 1 million street and traffic signs, it's small wonder that the city's construction crews are constantly busy maintaining and updating area roadways.

CALGARY

CALGARY HAS COME A LONG WAY SINCE its first recorded fire broke out in 1885. No fire department had yet been established, and residents tossed snowballs and pailfuls of water at the flames to extinguish them. Today, the Calgary Fire Department is made up of more than 1,000 men and women who respond to thousands of emergency calls each year.

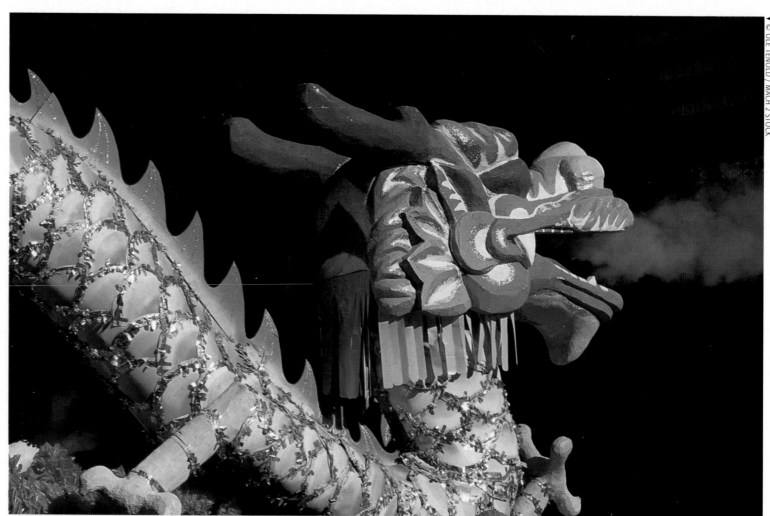

C A L G A R Y

Roland E-96

CHINESE CALGARIANS TAKE TO THE streets in a rich pageant of traditional costumes, music, and dance. Standing in the heart of Chinatown, the $10 million Calgary Chinese Cultural Centre (PAGES 202 AND 203) houses a non-profit organization that includes a cultural museum and a Chinese-language library. The blue ceramic tiles on the roof were made by the same company that produced the roof tiles for the Temple of Heaven in Beijing.

IERCELY DETERMINED TO PAY TRIBUTE to the achievements of Alberta's Chinese residents, two stone lions guard Sien Lok Park along Riverfront Avenue. Fighters of another sort, twins Keith and Colin Morgan of Calgary have both represented Canada's judo team in the Olympic Games—Colin in 1996, and Keith in 1996 and 2000.

善樂公園

SIEN LOK
PARK

CALGARY

F ROM ITS MODESTLY APPORTIONED dwellings to its million-dollar houses, Calgary is home to more than 800,000 people, each of whom possesses a unique sense of style.

HINING UNDER CALGARY'S FAMED blue skies, or basking in an electric glow, the Calgary area's many houses of worship extend an open invitation to residents (PAGES 210-215).

CALGARY

T HE UNIVERSITY OF CALGARY'S MORE THAN
60 academic departments and programs
run the gamut from undergraduate
degrees through PhDs. Mirroring its 30,000
students' ambition, the university's research
funding exceeds $134 million each year.

C A L G A R Y

THERE'S NO SHORTAGE OF ACADEMIC seeds in Calgary, as the University of Calgary's Garden of Learning (TOP) indicates. Mount Royal College (BOTTOM) offers certificate, diploma, and degree programs, and celebrated its 90th anniversary during the 2000-2001 academic year. At the Southern Alberta Institute of Technology (OPPOSITE), initially founded as the Alberta Provincial Institute of Technology and Art in 1916, students can take advantage of customized business and industry training.

C A L G A R Y

OMETIMES THE NEED TO RELAX takes precedence over all else (PAGES 220-223). Whether a walk along the Bow River or a multigenerational meandering strikes your fancy, Calgary shovels out a plenitude of opportunities for recreation.

THE GLASS OF FASHION AND THE
mould of form: from storefronts to
sidelines, urbanites and cowboys alike
find Calgary a suitable place to call home.

HEART OF THE NEW WEST   **225**

CALGARY

From Calgary's peaceful park benches and cold, clear streams to its reflective, elegant skyline, Calgarians and visitors can feel, anywhere in the city, the beating of the heart of the new west (PAGES 225-231).

Profiles in Excellence

A look at the corporations, businesses, professional groups, and community service organizations that have made this book possible. Their stories— offering an informal chronicle of the local business community—are arranged according to the date they were established in the Calgary area.

1886 Buffalo Café

Agrium Inc.

Alberta Blue Cross

Alberta Energy Company Ltd.

Avmax Group Inc.

The Banff Centre

Bank of Montreal

Bow Valley College

Cadillac Fairview Corporation Limited

Calgary Herald

Calgary Inc.

Calgary International Airport

Calgary Olympic Development Association

The Calgary Sun

The Calgary Zoo

Canada Safeway Limited

CFCN Television

Cisco Systems Canada Co.

Compaq Canada Inc.

Corus Radio Calgary

Crape Geomatics Corporation

Cybersurf Corporation

DeVry Institute of Technology

Dow Chemical Canada Inc.

Earth Tech Canada Inc.

Enerflex Systems Ltd.

Engage Energy

Fugro/SESL Geomatics Ltd.

Global Television Network

Hi-Tech Assembly Systems Inc.

ING Western Union Insurance Company

JORO Manufacturing Company Ltd.

Lafarge Canada Inc.

Mantei's Transport Ltd.

Marsh Canada, Limited

Media One Communications Limited

Merrill Lynch

Metso Automation

Mount Royal College

Nexen Inc.

NovAtel Inc.

Oxford Properties Group Inc.

Pillar Resource Services Inc.

QSound Labs, Inc.

Remington Development Corporation

Resorts of the Canadian Rockies - Skiing Louise Ltd.

RNG Pro-Tech Inc.

Sabre Energy Ltd.

Sanmina Canada ULC

SMART Technologies Inc.

Top Notch Construction Ltd.

TransAlta

Trico Homes Inc.

Trimac Corporation

UMA Engineering Ltd.

University of Calgary

Utilicorp Networks Canada

VECO Canada Ltd.

WDC Mackenzie Distributors Limited

Wingenback Inc.

xwave

Profiles in Excellence

Calgary Herald

Two Ontario adventurers set out in 1883 to find opportunity in the western frontier: Teacher Thomas Braden arrived in Calgary just ahead of the Canadian Pacific Railway and waited for his friend Andrew M. Armour, a printer who brought a hand press with him on the first train to arrive in the frontier town. And so begins the story of the *Calgary Herald.* ✿ Braden and Armour's fledgling newspaper, then called the *Calgary Herald, Mining and Ranche*

Advocate and General Advertiser, made history as one of the first three companies to set up business in Calgary. The paper's first four-page issue hit the streets in 1883.

As Calgary grew, so did the *Herald,* helping people stay informed and helping businesses prosper. Nearly 100 years later, in 1981, riding the coattails of the energy boom, the *Herald* built a new, $70 million publishing plant off of Deerfoot Trail on a bluff overlooking the city's burgeoning skyline. In 1987, the *Herald* again made history by becoming one of the first companies in Canada to establish an on-site day-care centre for staff members.

THE *Calgary Herald* PARTNERS WITH A NUMBER OF PROMINENT COMMUNITY ORGANIZATIONS, INCLUDING THE CALGARY FLAMES HOCKEY CLUB, THE UNIVERSITY OF CALGARY, SPRUCE MEADOWS, THE CALGARY HEALTH TRUST, AND OF COURSE THE WORLD FAMOUS CALGARY STAMPEDE.

The Herald Today

The *Herald* has always been viewed as one of the city's corporate icons. The paper has weathered the boom and bust trends of past economies, but, like the city it serves, the *Herald* has ben-

efited from the stability created by Calgary's more diversified economy.

Embracing the latest technological advances, the *Herald* is an industry leader in the production and design areas of the newspaper business. The *Herald* was the world's first major newspaper to use digital cameras that allow a photo to be processed and placed on a page within minutes of being taken by a photographer. The *Herald*'s

first fully digital edition was produced in 1995.

"Your City—Your Paper"

Newspapers such as the *Calgary Herald* play a unique role in their community. The job of any newspaper is first and foremost to attract readers by serving their needs—a considerable undertaking and responsibility not taken lightly by the editors, columnists, and reporters involved at the *Herald.*

"Our goal is to hold a mirror up to the community we serve," says Editor-in-Chief Peter Menzies. "We report events about the world around us in a way that is relevant and meaningful. That doesn't mean people will always like what they read, but we're dedicated to truthful and balanced reporting, and providing opinion and analysis from all points on the ideological spectrum.

"We have a vibrant, curious staff who understand and investigate the city and southern Alberta," Menzies continues. "There are more staff people in our newsroom than in virtually all the other media outlets in the city. We set the news agenda in this city, recognizing we live in a community that has high expectations of us and of itself."

Where Calgary Clicks

Calgary Herald Online is one of the busiest news and information sites in the country. Aside from offering current news, features, weather, and classified listings, the *Herald*'s Web site offers a full suite of interactive tools to guide users through the Calgary experience. An on-line

restaurant guide, movie listings, and an events data base are just a sampling of the attractions available on the paper's Web site.

Publishing a glossy magazine was something the *Herald* had never attempted before, but the paper's management saw an opportunity and seized it. *Western Legend* was launched in partnership with the Calgary Exhibition in July 1999. The magazine's articles and photography spotlight the entrepreneurial spirit and romance of the West, including art, cuisine, fashion, home styles, and profiles of leading-edge Calgarians. Published quarterly, *Western Legend* is distributed to approximately 95,000 Calgarians through selected editions of the *Calgary Herald* and through the mail. Another 10,000 copies are distributed or sold at the Stampede in July.

"Calgary and the southern part of our province are truly western areas, with a way of life all their own," says *Herald* President and Publisher Dan Gaynor. "When it became clear that the unique lifestyle of our region deserved a magazine showcasing it, we took the bull by the horns and produced our own."

Community Partnerships and Recognition

In addition to partnering with the Stampede, the *Herald* also partners with a number of other prominent organizations, including the Calgary Flames Hockey Club and Flames Foundation, the University of Calgary, Spruce Meadows, and the Calgary Health Trust.

The *Calgary Herald* Christmas fund contributes to a variety of Calgary charities and non-profit organizations. Since 1991, more than $3.8 million has been raised.

The *Herald* continues to receive accolades from colleagues and others. The American Inland Press Association awarded the *Herald* two prizes in its North American special sections competition in 1999 and 2000. The *Herald* also won the Calgary Board of Education's Lighthouse Awards 2000 in support of educational programming, the Mayor's Excellence Awards 2000 for a business-person contributing most to education, and the TransAlta Andy Russell Nature Writers Award for a series on the Bow River in 1998.

"Our newspaper is as distinct as the city it serves," says Gaynor. "Because our product cycle is daily, each and every day we have a new chance to ensure that we meet the expectations of our readers." With such a true Calgarian can-do attitude, the *Calgary Herald* will certainly continue to increase its loyal readership and to make history in the coming years.

THE *CALGARY HERALD* HAS BEEN FIRST ON THE SCENE IN LOCAL NEWS SINCE 1883. IT WAS FIRST TO OFFER ON-THE-SPOT COVERAGE OF THE JULY 2000 TORNADO THAT RAVAGED A PINE LAKE CAMPGROUND IN CENTRAL ALBERTA.

PEACE AND QUIET CAN BE FOUND JUST MOMENTS FROM THE CALGARY CITY LIMITS.

Bank of Montreal

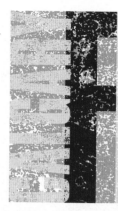

Founded in 1817, Bank of Montreal was the first bank in Canada. The bank was also the first bank in Calgary, opening a branch there in 1886. Calgary's first city fathers sent Colonel James Walker east to Montreal to ask for local banking facilities for the town, which in time would come to be known as the commercial centre of the new Northwest. 🍁 Today, Bank of Montreal is a highly diversified financial services institution, operating 32 lines of business within its group of companies, including BMO Nesbitt Burns, one of Canada's largest full-service investment firms and Chicago-based Harris Bank, a major U.S. midwestern financial institution.

Strong Calgary Presence

Since moving to Calgary, Bank of Montreal has developed and still maintains a strong presence in the city, with more than 20 full-service branches and seven branches located in Safeway stores. In Calgary, the bank maintains more than 100 InstaBank machines—Calgary was the city where ATM and debit machines were first piloted—and also operates one of three national call centres for telephone banking.

The city is also home to the bank's divisional headquarters for the prairie region, covering the provinces of Manitoba and Saskatchewan, as well as Alberta. The bank employs almost 1,000 Calgarians—some 450 in the branches, 250 in the mbanx Direct group (telephone banking), and 150 in other support groups or affiliated companies.

Even in the 21st century, Bank of Montreal is still pioneering. For example, the bank received the Institutional Shareholder Services 1999 International Best Practices Award for corporate governance. "Shareholders, investors, and analysts depend on us to deliver an effective system of governance based on transparency, as well as the timely and accurate disclosure of information," says Ted McCarron, Senior Vice-President, Prairies Division. "We're proud to be considered among the world's best."

Bank of Montreal has also been recognized with a number of investor relations awards, including the Award of Excellence for Leadership in Corporate Governance by the Canadian Institute of Chartered Accountants and the National Post in 1999. The bank won the 1998 *Investor Relations Magazine* Canada Award for having corporate governance policies that best reflect the interests of its shareholders. Bank of Montreal also ranked sixth in a field of 25 in The Globe and Mail's sixth annual ranking of Canada's most respected corporations.

BMO Nesbitt Burns

BMO Nesbitt Burns, one of Bank of Montreal's group of companies, is also recognized as a leader in the areas of personal finance, investment research, investment banking, institutional equity, and capital markets. BMO Nesbitt Burns is one of Canada's leading full-service investment firms, serving the financial needs of individual, institutional, corporate, and government clients. The firm employs some 4,300 people in offices across Canada and in the United States, as well as in 10 international locations.

IN 1932, BANK OF MONTREAL ERECTED A NEW BUILDING ON THE SAME SITE AS ITS FIRST PREMISES, WHICH IT OCCUPIED UNTIL 1983 (LEFT).

BANK OF MONTREAL'S FIRST PERMANENT PREMISES IN CALGARY OPENED IN 1889, THREE YEARS AFTER THE BANK ESTABLISHED ITS FIRST CALGARY BRANCH (RIGHT).

More than 1,400 investment advisers in the BMO Nesbitt Burns Private Client Division draw on a broad range of products and services. In addition to traditional equities, fixed-income securities, and mutual funds, BMO Nesbitt Burns has developed an extensive and growing line of proprietary products.

The BMO Nesbitt Burns Investment and Corporate Banking Group is the leading underwriter of debt and equity issues in Canada. A team of more than 150 professionals worldwide offers clients the value of leading financial advisory services, including mergers and acquisitions; divestitures; public takeover bids; takeover defenses; fairness opinions and valuations; and restructurings and recapitalizations.

Through offices in North America, Europe, and Asia, the firm's Capital Markets Group serves the global needs of many domestic and international clients through a wide range of fixed-income products.

The firm's Institutional Equity sales and trading team is the top trader and distributor of Canadian equities around the world. With significant capabilities outside of Canada, BMO Nesbitt Burns has achieved the largest market share in all major international markets for Canadian equities.

With a team of 32 analysts located in Toronto, Montreal, Calgary, and New York, the firm's Equities Research department covers more than 400 stocks across diverse sectors, and provides equity strategy, quantitative analysis, and portfolio management

services to BMO Nesbitt Burns' clients. "We are committed to becoming the premier Canadian investment firm in North America with a significant presence in Europe and Asia, and Calgary continues to be an extremely important market for our Investment and Corporate Banking Group," says John Abbott, Executive Managing Director, Investment and Corporate Banking, BMO Nesbitt Burns.

Community Involvement

Bank of Montreal and BMO Nesbitt Burns are also committed to their presence in Calgary. "We've always believed we have a responsibility to be active participants in each of the hundreds of communities in Canada where

we do business," says McCarron.

Bank of Montreal and BMO Nesbitt Burns have made a significant contributions to the Calgary community. Beneficiaries include the Calgary Regional Health Authority, University of Calgary, Mount Royal College, Kerby Centre, South Fish Creek Recreation Complex, Fort Calgary, HAWCS (police helicopter), United Way, STARS (Shock Trauma Air Rescue Society), and Calgary Stampede. "We've been the official bank for the Calgary Stampede for more than 100 years and, hopefully, many more centuries to come," says McCarron.

With a firmly rooted presence in Calgary and attention to service in business and the community, Bank of Montreal is truly a boon to the area.

FOR MORE THAN A CENTURY, BANK OF MONTREAL HAS BEEN THE OFFICIAL BANK OF THE GREATEST OUTDOOR SHOW ON EARTH, THE CALGARY EXHIBITION AND STAMPEDE (TOP).

ANNUALLY, A GROUP OF BANK OF MONTREAL EMPLOYEES CONSTRUCTS A PLAYHOUSE, WHICH IS RAFFLED OFF TO RAISE FUNDS FOR HABITAT FOR HUMANITY (BOTTOM LEFT AND RIGHT).

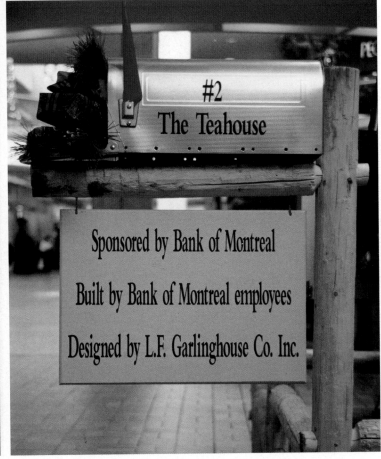

Sponsored by Bank of Montreal

Built by Bank of Montreal employees

Designed by L.F. Garlinghouse Co. Inc.

Earth Tech Canada Inc.

he Saddledome, LRT, Spruce Meadows, and Deerfoot Trail are all highly visible Calgary landmarks, but Earth Tech Canada Inc. (formerly Reid Crowther), the engineering company involved in these projects and many others, is also a local institution in its own right. The new millennium brought new opportunity–in 2000, Reid Crowther joined the Earth Tech group of companies. Reid Crowther has provided Canadian and inter-national clients with comprehensive water, transportation, building, and industrial engineering services for more than 90 years. Together with Earth Tech, its team now can apply greater technical and financial resources to providing solutions.

Reid Crowther's roots go back to pioneer times, when John Galt and his partner, Owen Smith, established an office in Calgary in 1906. With Galt's death a decade later, Edmund Miles and John Haddin took over the firm, and when it eventually merged with Davis and Associates, the name changed to Haddin, Davis & Brown Ltd. With the retirement of Haddin and the merger with Edmonton-based Crowther MacKay, Reid Crowther & Partners Ltd. was incorporated in Calgary in 1965. And although the company's name may have changed over the years, its skill, talent,

EARTH TECH CANADA INC., FORMERLY REID CROWTHER, PROVIDES HIGH-QUALITY CONSULTING, DESIGN, CONSTRUCTION, AND OPERATIONAL SERVICES TO MEET THE ENVIRONMENTAL AND INFRASTRUCTURE NEEDS OF INDUSTRY AND GOVERNMENT.

innovation, and expertise have remained quite consistent.

Itself founded in 1970, Earth Tech has become one of the leaders in engineering, environmental, construction, operations, and maintenance fields with more than 7,000 professionals in more than 130 offices worldwide. Earth Tech's mission is to provide high-quality consulting, design, construction, and operational services to meet the environmental and infrastructure needs of industry and government.

Innovative Wastewater Treatment

nnovation has always been an important aspect of our work," says Bill Berzins, Vice President. "One example of our ability is the Bonnybrook Wastewater Treatment Plant, which was the first plant in Canada to use thickened sludge to accelerate waste digestion. We introduced our client to this technology and encouraged its use. Envi-ronmental clubs give Calgary top marks in waste treatment because of that plant. It's still among the best in the world."

Another example of Earth Tech's innovation is Deerfoot Trail, one of the busiest transportation corridors in the province and one of the best flowing in Canada. "Deerfoot is one of the busiest arteries in western Canada, so we have worked together with both local and provincial authorities to achieve a balance between a high level of service and the most effective use of the taxpayer's investment in infrastructure," says Berzins.

"We're an international company and we recruit from all around the world. We're proud of our contribution to building Calgary and hundreds of communities around the world," says Berzins. Although the company name may change, by providing the highest-quality service to its local and international clients, Earth Tech Canada Inc. will remain a Calgary landmark for years to come.

stablished in 1910, Mount Royal College is one of Alberta's oldest and largest post-secondary educational institutions. From its three Calgary campuses, the college offers a variety of programs, including a collaborative bachelor of arts degree, applied baccalaureate degrees, university transfer, career diploma, and certificate programs. ❦ The college also has a world-renowned conservatory, which provides music and theatre instruction for all generations. More than 3,000 international

students choose Mount Royal each year for language training and credit programs. And the faculty of Continuing Education and Extension offer a diverse range of professional and personal development courses and programs.

"Our vision is to become Canada's leading undergraduate college, educating and training students for success in the new economy," says President Tom Wood.

Applied Degrees

Mount Royal pioneered the idea of applied bachelor degrees as a way of helping students succeed in the new knowledge-based economy. New applied degree programs are being added every year. So far, the college offers degrees in communication, business and entrepreneurship, child studies, interior design, justice studies, and policy studies. These programs integrate six semesters of course work with two semesters of paid work experience. Mount Royal collaborates with employers to arrange work term job postings.

"Students who graduate from these programs not only possess theoretical knowledge, but they also have hands-on experience in applying that knowledge," says Wood.

Mount Royal also offers a number of two-year diploma programs to prepare students for specific careers such as accounting, insurance, broadcasting, environmental technology,

and many more. Many of the diploma programs also offer work experience—sometimes paid—with potential employers.

The college recently introduced a bachelor of arts degree program as a joint effort with Athabasca University. Students who would previously have transferred to another institution can now complete their entire four-year program at Mount Royal. English, history, and psychology are offered, as is access to a broad range of support courses in many other arts and science disciplines.

For students pursuing other degrees, Mount Royal offers a two-year university transfer program. Students benefit from the personal attention and small class size at the college as they work toward their degree.

Learning Outcomes

Workers in the new economy need not only the basic skills to do the job, but also new employment skills. Mount Royal has developed a set of college-wide learning outcomes that will equip students with these abilities, such as communication skills, thinking skills, ethical reasoning, computer literacy, information retrieval and evaluation, and group effectiveness. These learning outcomes are being introduced into the college's courses and programs across the board.

Mount Royal is more than an innovative, progressive college with an excellent reputation. The instructors take a genuine interest in the development of each student, and because of the small class sizes, they have the time to evaluate each student's abilities and potential thoroughly.

Such personal attention pays off. More than 96 percent of graduates say they are satisfied with their experience at Mount Royal and 90 percent find jobs within six months of graduation. "Study today for the careers of tomorrow" is one of the college's slogans students can count on. With innovative degree programs and preparation for life after college, Mount Royal students will be poised for leadership in the years to come.

MOUNT ROYAL COLLEGE IS MORE THAN AN INNOVATIVE, PROGRESSIVE COLLEGE WITH AN EXCELLENT REPUTATION. "OUR VISION IS TO BECOME CANADA'S LEADING UNDERGRADUATE COLLEGE, EDUCATING AND TRAINING STUDENTS FOR SUCCESS IN THE NEW ECONOMY," SAYS PRESIDENT TOM WOOD.

TransAlta

ransAlta is an international electric energy company with more than $6.6 billion in assets. The company focuses exclusively on generation and transmission—where it has achieved a competitive edge as a low-cost operator—and is a successful gas-fired independent power project developer and energy marketer. TransAlta targets growth opportunities in both domestic and international deregulated markets. ☘ As a result of a newly

competitive energy market, the power industry is undergoing significant changes, and industry players are faced with new challenges and opportunities. TransAlta is emerging as an influential player with a clear vision and a strong presence both locally and internationally.

Providing electric energy in Alberta since 1911, the Calgary-based company has expanded with the growth and development of the province itself. Local water resources were first tapped with a number of small, hydroelectric plants. In later years—following the discovery of abundant, low-cost, low-sulphur coal reserves—larger, coal-fired plants were built to supply the province's growing electric power requirements. Throughout the years, Albertans have been fortunate to have abundant supplies of electric power at rates that are among the lowest in North America and the world.

BASED IN CALGARY SINCE ITS CREATION IN 1911, TRANSALTA'S HEAD OFFICE ACCOMMODATES MORE THAN 600 EMPLOYEES (TOP).

TRANSALTA IS A KEY CONTRIBUTOR TO THE EXTENSIVE REDEVELOPMENT OF THE CALGARY EXHIBITION AND STAMPEDE'S GRANDSTAND STAGE, WHICH INCLUDES CHANGES TO THE SOUND AND LIGHTING SYSTEMS ALONG WITH UNDERGROUND SUPPORT FACILITIES (BOTTOM).

Commitment to Sustainable Development and the Community

One of the ways TransAlta differentiates itself from its competitors is through its long-term, ongoing commitment to sustainable development. Each year there is an open and frank accounting of the company's efforts, in terms of both its successes and its shortcomings.

TransAlta has achieved significant progress in reducing the environmental impact of its operations. For example, the company has exceeded its goal of reducing net greenhouse gases from Canadian operations to 1990 levels by 2000. "We're more than 3 million tons below 1990 levels, despite an increase of almost 9 percent in generation," says Steve Snyder, President and CEO. And during 1999, all of the company's Canadian coal-fired and hydro facilities' environmental management systems were enhanced to meet the International Standards Organization's (ISO) 14001 standard.

In late 1999, TransAlta launched Project Planet, an environmental initiative, which challenges schoolchildren across Alberta to come up with innovative ideas to improve their local environments. During its first year, more than 350 Alberta schoolchildren participated in the contest, and two schools and two individuals received assistance in making their ideas become a reality.

TransAlta believes that being a good corporate citizen is an important measure of success. An active retiree volunteer program and a strong annual United Way campaign are two of the company's most focused areas of community involvement in Calgary.

TransAlta's community investments in Calgary include "TransAlta's Wildlights" at the Calgary Zoo and the zoo's planned Tropical

Africa Pavilion. As well, for 10 days every July, the company sponsors "TransAlta Lights Up the Night" with a fireworks display, and presents world-class entertainment on the TransAlta Grandstand stage as part of the Calgary Exhibition and Stampede.

Increasing Action in the Global Marketplace

TransAlta is concentrating its growth in Canada, the United States, Australia, and, most recently, Mexico. "We have identified Mexico as an attractive market with excellent growth potential," says Snyder. "We are building on our competitive advantage with projects there that fit our risk profile to continue to deliver long-term earnings growth." In March 2000, TransAlta won its first competitive bid to build and operate a 250-megawatt, gas-fired power plant in Mexico.

With the recent acquisition of a 1,340-megawatt, coal-fired power plant and mine in the state of Washington, TransAlta now owns more than 8,000 megawatts of generation.

TransAlta's position as the world's third-most efficient generator and one of North America's best power plant operators certainly provides an advantage. One measure of that performance is the company's five-year average availability factor for its Canadian coal-fired units of 91 percent, compared to the North American average of 86.4 percent.

The company is the number one independent power producer in Canada and the second-largest independent supplier of power in Western Australia.

"Although our growth strategy includes looking at markets beyond Alberta, about half of our total generating capacity is still in our home province," says Snyder. "We have—and will always have—roots here. Calgary is where TransAlta grew up. It's the home of our head office and where most of our employees live. We want to be part of the progress that is Calgary. This city is so much like TransAlta—innovative, dynamic, growth oriented, and entrepreneurial. Calgary is an international city—and the centre of Canada's energy industry—well suited for a focused, growth company like ours."

AS A MAJOR SPONSOR OF "WILDLIGHTS," TRANSALTA HELPS THE CALGARY ZOO BOOST ITS ATTENDANCE LEVELS DURING THE WINTER MONTHS.

TRANSALTA HAS BEEN GENERATING ELECTRICITY IN ALBERTA SINCE 1911.

Canada Safeway Limited

ounded in 1929 as Safeway Stores Limited by Walter J. Kraft, Canada Safeway Limited today not only supplies customers with superior food and home goods at competitive prices, but also provides a comprehensive array of in-store services for a complete shopping experience. With three operating areas—Winnipeg, Alberta, and British Columbia—Canada Safeway now runs more than 200 stores, stretching from Thunder Bay, Ontario, to the Pacific Coast. ✦

In addition to being home to 28 stores, Calgary has been the company's headquarters since 1984. In 1994, all of the company's administrative functions were consolidated in a new corporate headquarters off Deerfoot Trail in the northeast part of the city. "Calgary is a central location in western Canada," says President and Chief Operating Officer Grant M. Hansen. "From here we have ease of distribution, whatever the mode of transportation."

Local Purchases, Local Production

n an effort to maintain low prices without sacrificing quality, Canada Safeway operates its own manufacturing facilities, producing private label merchandise under brand names such as Safeway, Lucerne, and Safeway Select. These plants process ice cream, bread, frozen food, eggs, and frozen vegetables and fruit, as well as meat. With local processing plants, the company buys locally wherever possible. In fact, Canada Safeway is the largest buyer of local produce in western Canada.

The Calgary meat plant is considered state of the art and has Hazard Analysis Critical

Control Point (HACCP) certification, which ensures all procedures are governed by the most effective food safety standard and that products can be traced from the time they enter the plant until they leave. The tracking system allows the company to immediately pinpoint any problem and where in the processing stage it occurred. The same commit-

ment to health and safety can be seen in the stores themselves. Special auditors regularly visit each store to ensure proper food safety and sanitation procedures are employed, correct product temperatures are maintained, and prices are accurate.

Specialty departments and special services are now available in many stores, including china, kitchens, Starbucks, dry cleaning, photo processing centres, and Bank of Montreal (BMO) branches with a full range of banking services. "We try to provide one-stop shopping for today's busy customer," says Hansen.

A History of Innovation

ver since the company's earliest years, Safeway has been known for innovation. Free delivery was available in the early 1930s, but once the automobile became popular, Safeway was among the first to provide parking spaces and shopping carts for self-service. Other innovations in those years included pricing fruits and vegetables by the pound, special merchandising events, more-sanitary milk transportation, and a guaranteed meat-trim program that is still in effect today. The company also pioneered frozen food when it introduced its private label Bel Air frozen peas.

One recent innovation, which can be found in the North Hill and Crowfoot Towne Centre stores, is the concept of a natural foods store-within-a-store. In this case, a

FOUNDED IN 1929 AS SAFEWAY STORES LIMITED BY WALTER J. KRAFT, CANADA SAFEWAY LIMITED TODAY NOT ONLY SUPPLIES CUSTOMERS WITH SUPERIOR FOOD AND HOME GOODS AT COMPETITIVE PRICES, BUT ALSO PROVIDES A COMPREHENSIVE ARRAY OF IN-STORE SERVICES FOR A COMPLETE SHOPPING EXPERIENCE.

1,200-square-foot natural foods centre offers a wider choice of nutrition products. A natural medicine pharmacist is on staff and counsels shoppers on natural remedies and diet. In addition, a touch screen computer system, Health On-Line, provides interactive information on medicines, diets, and foods. A recently opened gas bar at Crowfoot Towne Centre offers further convenience for shoppers.

Safeway is also exploring a variety of alliances within the Internet community. The company has joined forces with more than 16 worldwide retailers to establish a worldwide retail exchange. As a Web-based marketplace, the exchange is designed to facilitate and simplify trading between retailers and more than 100,000 suppliers, partners, and distributors.

A third alliance has been developed with GroceryWorks.com, a leading Dallas-based on-line home fulfilment business specializing in groceries. GroceryWorks will serve as Safeway's exclusive on-line grocery channel. "To be successful in e-commerce, you need both the 'clicks' and the 'mortar,'" says Hansen. "GroceryWorks has the 'clicks' and we have the 'mortar.' We intend to offer customers the convenience of shopping in stores on-line."

Caring for the Community: A Safeway Tradition

Safeway not only nourishes the body, but also—as a good corporate citizen for more than 70 years—feeds the community spirit. Each year, Safeway contributes to more than 2,000 community groups and organizations by providing equipment or employee volunteers, or by donating cash and in-kind merchandise. Hundreds of non-profit groups increase their viability through in-store programs such as Lucerne milk cartons, community bulletin boards, and brochure distribution.

In 1999, Safeway's western Canada employees raised more than $1 million for 200 causes across the country through the Because We Care in-store charity challenge. By holding hot dog sales, garage sales, barbecues, book sales, and other activities, one of the Calgary stores raised almost $10,000 for a scholarship in memory of Clayton McGloan, a well-respected and popular student who was killed trying to break up a fight. In addition, store employees have supported causes in Calgary, including the Shock Trauma Air Rescue Society (STARS), Alberta Children's Hospital, Calgary Women's Shelter, and many more.

The company's commitment to innovation and community involvement is a formula that has stood the test of time. Safeway's trademark red S was unveiled in 1952. Since then the S has gone on to become one of the most recognized brands in North America, and is an important part of Calgary's history as well as of its future.

A NATURAL MEDICINE PHARMACIST IS ON STAFF AND COUNSELS SHOPPERS ON NATURAL REMEDIES AND DIET.

IN AN EFFORT TO MAINTAIN LOW PRICES WITHOUT SACRIFICING QUALITY, CANADA SAFEWAY OPERATES ITS OWN MANUFACTURING FACILITIES, PRODUCING PRIVATE LABEL MERCHANDISE UNDER BRAND NAMES SUCH AS SAFEWAY, LUCERNE, AND SAFEWAY SELECT.

The Banff Centre

Nestled in the Canadian Rockies, a short drive from Calgary, The Banff Centre is Canada's only learning centre for the arts, leadership development, and mountain culture. With an expanding vision that encompasses lifelong learning, The Banff Centre offers leading-edge educational opportunities, as well as a wide range of unique experiences for visitors, tourists, and local Albertans. 🍁 The Banff Centre is also a world-class conference

WITH AN EXPANDING VISION THAT ENCOMPASSES LIFELONG LEARNING, THE BANFF CENTRE OFFERS LEADING-EDGE EDUCATIONAL OPPORTUNITIES, AS WELL AS A WIDE RANGE OF UNIQUE EXPERIENCES FOR VISITORS, TOURISTS, AND LOCAL ALBERTANS.

facility. Located in a serene mountain setting, the Centre is situated on more than 40 acres of forest and trails overlooking the town of Banff. The site features more than 60 meeting rooms, an art gallery, two theatres, teaching studios, and auditoriums that accommodate from 10 to 1,000 people. More than 400 single bedrooms are available, each with a private bath. A new, lodge-style building features superior, four-star accommodations. The dining room, with its floor-to-ceiling windows offering a panoramic view of the Bow Valley, seats 480 people.

Among the guest services and numerous recreation opportunities available are a multilingual staff; room service; an executive chef providing customized menus and banquet themes; and a full-service recreational facility, including an exercise and weight room, gymnasium, indoor running track, indoor swimming pool, whirlpool, aerobics classes, massage, fitness appraisals, and nutrition consultation. The Centre also offers cultural and heritage opportunities such as art walks, concerts, performances, and exhibitions.

Early Years

The Banff Centre was originally launched in 1933 as a summer drama school. Each year, it grew in size and scope, offering programs in a wide variety of arts disciplines, to become a world-renowned international retreat for artists.

From a fine arts institution in 1970, The Banff Centre changed its focus to continuing education, and broadened its program areas for customers and their changing needs. The Alberta Government granted the Centre full

SCOTT ROWED

DONALD LEE

DONALD LEE

autonomy as a non-degree-granting educational institute in 1978.

In the 1950s, a school for management and leadership development was added, and today, the Centre is also home to an international conference facility and the dynamic Centre for Mountain Culture.

Current Mandate

The Banff Centre, through the leadership of current President and CEO Dr. Graeme McDonald, has moved beyond providing traditional education. The advent of the information age has clarified the need for ongoing professional development. And, as the population ages and baby boomers head toward retirement, personal growth and development have taken on increased emphasis in society. The Banff Centre prides itself on meeting the needs of today's lifelong learners.

Participants at The Banff Centre are generally mid-career professionals, who will often make multiple trips to the Centre throughout their professional lives. For artists, the Centre for the Arts still represents a retreat where they can either focus on their work with no disruptions, or collaborate with peers and mentors. Many short courses and symposiums focus on cutting-edge trends and skill development, particularly in the area of new media.

Within the Centre for Management, business, government, and community leaders focus on building sustainable leadership skills that lead to transformational behaviour in both their personal and their professional lives. The management division has also moved, with great success, to designing and implementing customized leadership development programs for organizations and institutions seeking immediate impact and a competitive edge.

The Centre for Mountain Culture provides a forum for the artistic, cultural, scientific, and recreational issues related to the mountain community. It promotes an understanding and lifelong appreciation of the world's mountain places through programs such as the Banff Mountain Film and Book festivals, international photography competition, and grants programs.

The Centre for Conferences has also embraced the values of lifelong learning. Conference guests, already enamoured with the Centre's retreatlike environment and lodge-style guest rooms, continually expressed interest in the working side of the Centre, particularly in the areas of the arts and mountain culture. In response, in 1999, the Centre launched the Live & Learn Series, a number of short- and longer-term learning vacations that connect travelers to Banff's

culture, nature, and people. From music appreciation to backstage tours, and from grizzly bear research to photography and mountain exploration workshops, participants can choose from a variety of cultural and heritage themes. For example, through the Centre's partnership with *National Geographic,* one learning holiday offers the opportunity to hike and learn photography with some of the world's best adventure photographers.

Building on the Banff Centre's past legacy, McDonald has positioned the Centre to continue to be a valued resource in Alberta's backyard. "Whether you want to attend a concert and stay overnight, host your company's annual meeting, or participate in one of our professional development programs, there is something for everyone," says McDonald. "We encourage Albertans to take advantage of all we have to offer and to experience The Banff Centre."

THOUGH ORIGINALLY LAUNCHED IN 1933 AS A SUMMER DRAMA SCHOOL, THE BANFF CENTRE IS A WORLD-CLASS CONFERENCE FACILITY THAT FEATURES MORE THAN 60 MEETING ROOMS, AN ART GALLERY, TWO THEATRES, TEACHING STUDIOS, AND AUDITORIUMS THAT ACCOMMODATE FROM 10 TO 1,000 PEOPLE.

 ▲ DONALD LEE

▲ BRIAN HARDER

▲ DONALD LEE

Calgary International Airport

Calgary International Airport is much more than a place to catch a plane. It's a gathering place that reflects the nature and the values of a very special, forward-thinking, dynamic city. It's also one of the lowest-cost major airports in Canada. The Calgary Airport Authority has 135 full-time staff employed to serve a facility that handles approximately 8 million passengers a year. ✦

"We have an outstanding group of employees," says Julien De Schutter, vice president of airport marketing. "They have a unique, single-minded focus on serving customers. Calgary Airport Authority employees are a part of the many 'partners in the pursuit of excellence' that make up the airport community of tenants, contractors, concession and other service providers—all with the common goal of providing a safe, efficient, and friendly total airport experience."

In addition, the airport is fortunate to have the services of 177 White Hat volunteers. Founded in 1991 by Elizabeth Wesley, manager hospitality relations, these volunteers perform the official White Hat Welcome ceremony, assist with VIP escorts, conduct airport tours, and participate in greeting delegates to the numerous conventions held in Calgary and Banff. Dressed in the traditional white hat and red vests, these volunteers are often the first smiling face introducing visitors to the Calgary spirit.

"CALGARY INTERNATIONAL AIRPORT IS RECOGNIZED WORLDWIDE AS AN INDUSTRY INNOVATOR. WHEN OTHERS WANT TO KNOW THE FUTURE OF AIRPORTS, THEY COME TO US," SAYS JULIEN DESCHUTTER, VICE PRESIDENT OF AIRPORT MARKETING.

Calgary Airport Authority

The history of the Calgary International Airport dates back to 1939. The original terminal building from those early years is still in use by an airport tenant. In 1977, a new terminal complex was opened. More than 20 years later, the facility is still highly regarded for its functionality and design.

Following negotiations with the Canadian government, the responsibility to manage the Calgary International Airport was transferred to the Calgary Airport Authority in 1992. The Authority is a not-for-profit corporation with a long-term lease of the airport lands in north-east Calgary, as well as the general aviation and flight training facility at Springbank, just west of the city. The Authority is mandated to manage and operate the airports in a safe, secure, and efficient manner, as well as to advance economic and community development.

The Authority's key strategic directions are laid out in its current business plan: to maximize the airport's potential as an intermodal hub; to pursue service and value excellence in cooperation with the airport's partners; to develop airport lands for uses that are compatible to airport operations and add value to the airport; to promote economic growth through tourism development; and to partner with the community to develop programs that enhance the quality of life.

New Access and Land Development

Calgary International Airport has a total land base of 5,070 acres, including 1,800 acres of land that are not required for airport operations. In 1998, the Authority implemented a new land development strategy with the intent of expanding tourism opportunities and attracting high-tech businesses to on-site business parks. The Authority is also studying the possibility of developing e-commerce, with the establishment of a centralized distribution and inventory centre for Internet retailers.

In addition to the ongoing expansion of the airfield and the air terminal complex to accommodate continuing growth, the Authority is participating in a unique four-way partnership to construct a new access road, Airport Trail, to alleviate traffic congestion, and to connect the terminal directly to Highway 2/Deerfoot Trail.

Inside the airport terminal, passengers and local residents are delighted with the recent expansion of retail services, with many new food and beverage outlets, as well as unique shops, each fully committed to street pricing. All airport retailers must demonstrate that their prices are no higher than comparable products and services at off-airport locations.

The shops attract local browsers, but families with children will especially want to check out SpacePort. Officially opened in September 2000, this free-of-charge, 6,000-square-foot interactive education and entertainment centre on the mezzanine level of the terminal is an attraction to travelers, as well as a destination for Calgary families. At SpacePort, visitors have the chance to truly experience space, flight, and high-tech communications. SpacePort even features a one-quarter-scale aluminum prototype of the NASA space shuttle *Orbiter*.

"It was offered by NASA on long-term loan," says Myrna Dubé, project director for SpacePort and director of tourism and community development. "It's built to an exacting level of detail, and it's really going to give people a fantastic opportunity to see exactly what a shuttle is like."

A Priority on Community Involvement

Adding value to the community requires more than excellent passenger and aircraft facilities.

For example, through Attractions Alberta, a partnership with 41 tourism and economic development organizations, space is provided within the terminal building to showcase regional tourism attractions.

Phase one of another project—the Airport Parkway—was completed in 1997, with a six-kilometre pathway linking the airport with the city's extensive pathway network. The Authority plans to raise funds to develop a series of parks along the pathway. In addition, a portion of the airport's lands has been set aside for the development of the Rotary Challenger Park. "Calgary needs a recreation

facility devoted to athletes with special needs," says Dubé. "The Authority has agreed to provide 16 acres for a barrier-free park that will include softball and baseball facilities, and later a soccer field, track, lawn bowling, and other facilities. Calgary's Rotary Clubs have banded together to champion this project and raise the funds to make it happen."

"Our long-term development plan has been enthusiastically endorsed by all the airlines," says De Schutter. "Our airport is recognized worldwide as an industry innovator. When others want to know the future of airports, they come to us."

THE WHITE HAT VOLUNTEERS—FOUNDED IN 1991 BY ELIZABETH WESLEY—ARE THE FIRST CONTACT TO EXTEND THE CALGARY SPIRIT BY MEETING AND GREETING ARRIVING PASSENGERS AND HELPING THEM AROUND THE TERMINAL BUILDING. THEY PERFORM THE HONOURARY CALGARIAN WHITE HAT WELCOME CEREMONY, ASSIST WITH VIP ESCORTS, CONDUCT AIRPORT TOURS, AND PARTICIPATE IN GREETING CONVENTION DELEGATES.

AT SPACEPORT, VISITORS HAVE THE CHANCE TO TRULY EXPERIENCE SPACE, FLIGHT, AND HIGH-TECH COMMUNICATIONS. SPACEPORT EVEN FEATURES A ONE-QUARTER-SCALE ALUMINUM PROTOTYPE OF THE NASA SPACE SHUTTLE *Orbiter*.

ING Western Union Insurance Company

NG Western Union Insurance Company traces its roots back to 1940, when it was founded by a prominent Calgary businessman. Starting out as a family-owned business, ING Western Union is now one of the largest and most successful property and casualty insurance companies in western Canada. ✦ "ING Western Union has established itself as a major player in the western Canadian insurance market," says Derek Iles, President and Chief Operating Officer. "We have built a solid reputation for providing responsive customer service, superior claims services, and an expanding range of insurance products to meet the needs of consumers."

Through innovative growth, mergers, acquisitions, and sound financial management, ING Western Union has grown to more than $600 million in assets and employs close to 600 people. Headquartered in Calgary, the company has regional offices in Edmonton, Calgary, Victoria, and Vancouver.

Products and Services

Over the years, ING Western Union has continued to build upon its line of personal and business insurance products and services. Today, the firm's customers can access a diverse range of insurance products for their automobile, home and personal property, business, farm, condominium, recreational vehicles, and watercraft.

ING Western Union's customers also benefit from unique product offerings such as the Personal Insurance Protector, which combines personal property and auto insurance in a single policy at lower cost and with improved coverage.

Sound Partnerships

ING Western Union's products and services are delivered to consumers through a network of independent insurance brokers and other insurance intermediaries in Alberta, British Columbia, Saskatchewan, the Northwest Territories, Yukon, and Nunavut.

The company also seeks out other alliances as well. For example, ING Western Union has formed a relationship with the British Columbia Automobile Association to provide its members another choice for purchasing auto insurance, underwritten by ING Western Union.

"Staying close to the local market ensures

ING Western Union Insurance Company is headquartered in the heart of Calgary (left).

ING Western Union and Calgary farrier Steve Woodall represent the best of the region's western heritage (right).

ANGUS OF CALGARY

MARIANNE RIDDLE

that we understand and can respond quickly to what our customers want and need," says Iles. "One way we can do this is to involve our brokers in Broker Advisory Councils, set up specifically for this purpose."

Commitment to Community

NG Western Union is proud of its western roots and its close ties with the community. Each year, the company contributes financially and with personnel resources to support community safety initiatives, including crime prevention, fire, and traffic safety public awareness programs.

ING Western Union currently sponsors a smoke detector installation and maintenance program, as well as a fire and burn prevention program that teaches children how to react in a fire emergency. The company also supports community-based traffic safety initiatives and the Rural Crime Watch Program. "When we partner with community groups, we are able to give something back to the community and local economy, while helping to make the community a safer, more vibrant place in which to live", says Iles.

In addition, the company takes a very active interest in education, supporting insurance programs at the University of Calgary and Mount Royal College in Calgary, and Grant MacEwan College in Edmonton. ING Western Union representatives sit on advisory committees, helping to develop educational curriculum for these programs and assisting in student job placement.

Across the Country, Around the World

While its roots are firmly entrenched in western Canada, ING Western Union is also a member of ING Group. One of the largest and most successful integrated financial services organizations in the world, ING Group has assets of more than $718 billion and employs more than 91,000 people in 60 countries.

Across Canada, ING Western Union affiliates include ING Canada, ING Halifax, ING Commerce Group, ING Novex, ING Wellington, BELAIRdirect, and ING Direct. Together, these companies form a network of Canadian businesses with a solid history of leadership and innovation. They offer an ever expanding range of insurance, financial security, and wealth-building solutions to customers across the country. Across North America, this network includes more than 20 companies and close to 10,000 employees aligned under the ING Group brand.

"This unique relationship provides us with the support and backing of a strong financial performer, while enabling us to focus on the local market," says Iles. "This arrangement makes it easier than ever for our customers to access ING expertise, and a wide range of insurance, banking, and asset management services."

Looking to the Future

In little more than 60 years, ING Western Union has grown from a small, family business to one of the largest organizations of its kind in western Canada. "To stay on top, we need to be innovative in delivering the types of products, services, and support our brokers and customers need," Iles says. "We also need to continually seek new opportunities for growth in the markets where we do business."

For ING Western Union, the future is bright. The company—whose vision is to be "first in products, first in service, first in relationships, and first in results"—intends to continue strengthening relationships with brokers, enhancing product distribution channels, creating new alliances, using technology effectively, and reducing operating costs. "Western Canadians like to deal with a western company," says Iles. "We're proud of our strong presence in Calgary, and plan to be part of the western Canadian community for many years to come."

IN LITTLE MORE THAN 60 YEARS, ING WESTERN UNION HAS GROWN FROM A SMALL, FAMILY BUSINESS TO ONE OF THE LARGEST ORGANIZATIONS OF ITS KIND IN WESTERN CANADA.

Alberta Blue Cross

n 1948, a small blue cross became the symbol of a bold new movement to help Albertans struggling with the daunting challenge of paying for medical care. Alberta Blue Cross began as a company dedicated solely to helping people pay their hospital bills in an era when universal health care did not exist. ❦ Alberta Blue Cross has been serving the Calgary area for more than 50 years. Alberta-based and -grown, the company is the province's leading provider of quality

supplementary health and dental benefits, as well as group life, disability, and emergency medical travel coverage. Independent and not-for-profit, Alberta Blue Cross serves more than 1.2 million Albertans through its government-sponsored, employer group, and individual plans. Last year alone, Alberta Blue Cross processed 16 million claims, valued at approximately $590 million.

The company takes its local roots very seriously. "We have offices throughout Alberta, and most of our employees were born and raised in the province," says Warren Pacaud, Manager of the Calgary office and Southern Alberta Group Sales. "As well, our board of directors is comprised of Albertans from all parts of the province and various walks of life." This Alberta focus sets Alberta Blue Cross apart from the rest of the industry, and helps the organization react quickly and responsively to the changing needs of its customers.

Unique Customer Base

lberta Blue Cross' unique regional customer base includes more than 3,000 employer-sponsored groups, half of which are located in Calgary and include some of the city's largest employers, such as the City of Calgary, Alberta Energy Company, Calgary Regional Health Authority, and the University of Calgary. Since group plans are available to organizations with as few as two employees, small businesses also have access to affordable group benefits that are often only obtainable by large employers.

Calgarians without employer-sponsored group benefits can purchase individual health and dental plans that meet their needs and budget, while Albertans travelling or studying outside Canada can choose an emergency medical plan. "The number of Calgary residents taking advantage of our individual

EXCEPTIONAL CUSTOMER SERVICE IS A CORE VALUE OF ALBERTA BLUE CROSS. STAFF RESPOND TO HUNDREDS OF INQUIRIES EACH DAY FROM CALGARY RESIDENTS.

plans is growing, as more people move into the city to start up their own businesses or to work on contract or on a consulting basis," says Pacaud.

Alberta Blue Cross also administers provincial, territorial, and federally sponsored health benefits programs. These include Alberta Health and Wellness's Palliative Care Coverage, Multiple Sclerosis Drug Coverage, Non-Group Coverage, and Coverage for Seniors, which provides premium-free coverage to more than 300,000 Alberta seniors for health-related expenses such as prescription drugs and ambulance trips.

Maximizing Technology

Alberta Blue Cross is continually using technology to help deliver the highest level of service. For example, all pharmacies in Calgary and across the province use Alberta Blue Cross' electronic claims system, PRIDE RT®, to process customer claims within seconds. Dental offices can also transmit claims in a similar manner. These systems allow service providers to bill Alberta Blue Cross directly, so that customers can simply show an ID card instead of paying for products and services up front. Using this technology significantly reduces administration and billing requirements, and simplifies the process for customers.

In addition, Alberta Blue Cross has one of the most advanced claims adjudication systems in North America. This state-of-the-art system is designed to process claims quickly and issue cheques promptly.

As well, the company's Web site, www.ab.bluecross.ca, allows customers and service providers to instantly access information about the organization and to download forms—saving time and resources for all parties.

Responding to Customer Needs

Because of its local presence and knowledge of Alberta's health care system, Alberta Blue Cross has been able to establish unique relationships with health service providers. For example, the company has agreements with Alberta pharmacies and ambulance operators to get the lowest possible prices for Alberta Blue Cross customers.

"We're proud of the fact that we listen and respond to our customers' needs," says Pacaud. "We receive more than half a million calls a year from our customers; you can always talk to someone at Alberta Blue Cross. We believe in face-to-face contact—and that personal touch."

At the heart of the company is innovation—developing new products to meet changing needs. Health spending accounts, for example, are available to groups of 10 employ-

ees or more. These accounts allow employees to use pretax dollars to pay for health and dental expenses not otherwise covered. The company's Benefit Plus product is specially tailored to the needs of small business. Also, LifeLink® is an innovative new product that protects employees in the event of a critical illness.

Supporting the Community

Alberta Blue Cross' personal touch extends to the communities it serves. Hearts of Blue, an employee-initiated and -run volunteer program, supports different local charities each year. Each Alberta Blue Cross office chooses which organizations to assist, and then raises funds and donates volunteer time and equipment. In Calgary, Agape Manor, the Emergency Women's Shelter, and the

Children's Cottage are among the recipients of this program.

The company is also proud of its scholarship program, initiated in 1998 to commemorate Alberta Blue Cross' 50th anniversary. A $1 million endowment will fund the program in perpetuity to provide entrance scholarships—based on academic achievement and financial need—to post-secondary students attending Alberta institutions, including the University of Calgary, Mount Royal College, and the Southern Alberta Institute of Technology (SAIT). Scholarships have also been created specifically for Aboriginal students and those with special needs.

As the health needs of Albertans evolve, Alberta Blue Cross will continue to listen to and meet the needs of its customers, playing a vital role in the Calgary community for many years to come.

THROUGH ITS OFFICE IN THE HEART OF DOWN-TOWN CALGARY, ALBERTA BLUE CROSS MAINTAINS STRONG TIES WITH THE LOCAL COMMUNITY (TOP).

BUILDING RELATIONSHIPS WITH BUSINESSES AND RESPONDING TO THEIR NEEDS IS A PRIORITY FOR ALBERTA BLUE CROSS. CORPORATE SALES REPRESENTATIVE DON FORBES, TOGETHER WITH SERVICE REPRESENTATIVE BREDA LENNOX (FAR RIGHT), WORKS CLOSELY WITH EMPLOYER GROUP PLAN ADMINISTRATORS SUCH AS SHIRLEY SISSON AND CAROLINE ARNIERI OF ALBERTA ENERGY COMPANY (BOTTOM LEFT).

ALBERTA BLUE CROSS IS HELPING YOUNG PEOPLE PURSUE THEIR DREAMS THROUGH ITS 50TH ANNI-VERSARY SCHOLARSHIP PROGRAM. LANA THOMAS, WHO IS STUDYING TO BECOME A TEACHER, WAS ONE OF THE FIRST RECIPIENTS OF ITS SCHOLARSHIPS FOR ABORIGINAL STUDENTS (BOTTOM RIGHT).

The Calgary Zoo

The Calgary Zoological Society was founded in 1929 as the first registered nonprofit society in Alberta. From its first small collection of animals, the zoo has evolved into a major attraction for Calgarians and visitors alike. ❧ In 1999, the Calgary Zoo welcomed more than 1 million visitors through its gates. Adults and children of all ages enjoyed the ever changing sights and sounds of a trip through nature nestled in the centre of a growing city.

Open 365 days a year, the Calgary Zoo hosts a number of special events that attract thousands of visitors. The zoo is recognized both locally and nationally, having received awards from Attractions Canada as the country's best outdoor site and the *Calgary Herald*'s Readers' Choice Award for the city's best attraction.

An Island of Learning

The Calgary Zoo has a number of fascinating and unique features. Located on the Bow River's St. George's Island, the zoo is only five minutes from downtown. "Because the zoo is accessible by light rail transit, many visitors don't even notice that it's on an island," says Calgary Zoo President and CEO Alex Graham. "Its proximity to downtown makes it easy for tourists to visit our island escape."

The Calgary Zoo is the only zoo in North America to house a Canadian wilds habitat, a prehistoric park, botanical gardens, and a collection of exotic animals on the same site. The zoo is enhancing its unique environment even further with its latest project: the creation of an actual African ecosystem, including the largest indoor gorilla exhibit in North America and an indoor, underwater river hippopotamus exhibit. The project, called Destination Africa, will also include an indoor tropical rain forest, plus an outdoor plains and grasslands area where a range of different species will share the same space—just as if they were in the wild.

The Calgary Zoo's Canadian wilds area is one of the only places in the world where indigenous plants and animals can be seen in accurate representations of their natural environment. "The Canadian wilds is an ideal place for tourists to visit before heading out to Banff," says Graham. "They get an excellent opportunity to see animals that are not always visible in the Rocky Mountains ecosystem."

The zoo's prehistoric park is also unique to the world. Within its 6.5 hectares, visitors can experience what western Canada might have been like when dinosaurs reigned supreme. Geologic formations, more than 100 plant species, and a collection of life-sized dinosaur models represent prehistoric times.

Finally, the Dorothy Harvie Gardens boasts a collection of more than 4,000 cultivated and native plant species in unique garden settings, including butterfly, palm, and arid gardens. "One of our goals is to test various species for suitability to Calgary's growing conditions, and provide information and inspiration for gardeners in the chinook zone," says Graham.

Education, conservation, and scientific study are important parts of the zoo's mission, and are woven into all of its activities. The zoo participates in managed breeding programs to help ensure the survival of endangered species. Outreach programs deliver environmental education to schools, seniors' homes, the media, community groups, and business associations, and assist in conservation projects worldwide. Conservation research projects at the Calgary Zoo include studying infertility in whooping cranes, a breeding program for Vancouver Island marmots, and researching mortality causes for Canada's most endangered carnivore, the swift fox.

"The Calgary Zoo is a community resource," says Graham. "We enhance the quality of life by helping Calgarians and visitors to the city maintain their links with nature. We invite the world to discover life on earth at the Calgary Zoo."

CLOCKWISE FROM TOP:

LOCATED AT THE CALGARY ZOO, THE DOROTHY HARVIE GARDENS BOAST A COLLECTION OF MORE THAN 4,000 CULTIVATED AND NATIVE PLANT SPECIES IN UNIQUE GARDEN SETTINGS, INCLUDING BUTTERFLY, PALM, AND ARID GARDENS.

WITHIN THE 6.5 HECTARES OF THE ZOO'S PREHISTORIC PARK, VISITORS CAN EXPERIENCE WHAT WESTERN CANADA MIGHT HAVE BEEN LIKE WHEN DINOSAURS REIGNED SUPREME.

THE ZOO'S CANADIAN WILDS AREA IS ONE OF THE ONLY PLACES IN THE WORLD WHERE INDIGENOUS PLANTS AND ANIMALS CAN BE SEEN IN ACCURATE REPRESENTATIONS OF THEIR NATURAL ENVIRONMENT.

Profiles in Excellence

1958

1969

Merrill Lynch

errill Lynch has a proud tradition that dates back to 1885, and it is this legacy that provides the company with a strong foundation for the exciting challenges of today's rapidly changing business environment. ❧ Since 1952, Merrill Lynch has been providing investment banking services to Canadians. With the acquisition of Midland Walwyn in 1998, Merrill Lynch established itself as a full-service brokerage firm

by extending its services to individual investors. With more than 3,000 employees across Canada, Merrill Lynch is uniquely positioned to offer to its clients world-class guidance and support.

With a total staff of 180, including 80 financial consultants, Merrill Lynch Canada's complex in Bow Valley Square serves as the backbone for Calgary's Private Client Group services, and is led by Jim Sorenson, Resident Vice President and Director, Private Client Group. In addition to the Calgary office, the company operates offices in Alberta in Lethbridge and Medicine Hat, as well as suboffices in Olds, Vulcan, Taber, Picture Butte, and Brooks.

"Merrill Lynch stands for strength and integrity, and we've been providing generation after generation of Canadians with top-rated financial information and investment guidance," says Sorenson. "We emphasize the development of long-term client relationships by anticipating their needs and offering them the broadest array of financial services available anywhere in the world."

Those services include financial planning, tax-advantaged investments, strategic asset allocation, asset management, education funding, international investments, and investment trusts, as well as retirement and estate planning. Merrill Lynch clients can choose from a variety of products, including mutual funds, segregated funds, equities, fixed-income products, and insurance.

Merrill Lynch is dedicated to providing sound financial services to clients in every economic bracket. According to Sorenson, "Whether you are a seasoned, affluent investor or a young professional opening your first RRSP account, you'll find what you need. We're really very broad based."

Global Presence, Local Expertise

o one dominates the pages of Merrill Lynch history like Charles E. Merrill. Early on, Merrill had some different ideas about the investment business, believing that market opportunities should be accessible to everyone. In 1914, when his name first appeared on a brass plate in New York City, Merrill set about his life's work of bringing Wall Street to Main Street.

Merrill Lynch expanded and diversified throughout the 1960s, becoming a publicly listed company in the United States in 1971. Although a Merrill Lynch office was established in Toronto in 1952, the Calgary operation was founded by Lock & Co. in 1945. Following a number of mergers and takeovers, Lock & Co. eventually became

SINCE 1952, MERRILL LYNCH HAS BEEN PROVIDING INVESTMENT BANKING SERVICES TO CANADIAN CLIENTS IN EVERY ECONOMIC BRACKET.

Midland Walwyn Inc., Canada's largest independent full-service securities firm. In 1998, Merrill Lynch acquired Midland Walwyn, including the Calgary office, to create Merrill Lynch Canada Inc.

"Since 1988, client assets in our complex have grown from $150 million to more than $3 billion," says Sorenson. "Being the only global firm operating in Canada, and with offices all over the world, we have a better understanding of various international markets. This enables us to help our clients make wiser investment decisions."

One of the core principles at Merrill Lynch is to conduct business in a way that always considers the human element. Built on the strong yet simple philosophy of putting clients' interests first, the modern day Merrill Lynch has a set of five principles that underlie everything the company does. These principles are client focus, respect for the individual, teamwork, responsible citizenship, and integrity.

"Our principles are not just a marketing slogan," says Sorenson. "They're not just something we've put on the office wall. They're something we live by."

The investment industry is currently in the throes of massive change. This is due in part to the growth of the Internet, which provides access to global markets and allows investors to make their own investment decisions on-line. Investors are becoming more educated, are participating in global markets personally and directly, and are more confident, intelligent, and better informed than ever before.

"We appreciate these changes, and we believe we provide real added value to investors through our reach, wisdom, and ability to sort through all of the options," says Sorenson. "We also have the discipline to stay focused on the client's financial plan. Clients choose their financial services provider with care. They establish the terms of the relationship, and we

acknowledge this by excelling in our client service."

Merrill Lynch customizes client relationships, depending on the individual's needs and desires. For some, that may mean meeting once a month to review their portfolio. For others, once a year is sufficient. The company's clients span a broad range of ages, proving that everyone can benefit from expert financial planning assistance, regardless of their stage in life.

"The essence of all that we do at Merrill Lynch begins with the human relationship," says Sorenson. "This commitment to personal service is the reason our financial consultants excel in delivering the wisdom and performance clients need to achieve their dreams."

Excellence, defined by lasting relationships instead of assets, is the approach that has defined Merrill Lynch's success. As the needs of clients change, the financial expertise of Merrill Lynch's professionals will become even more valuable in the years to come.

MERRILL LYNCH'S CLIENTS CAN CHOOSE FROM A VARIETY OF PRODUCTS, INCLUDING MUTUAL FUNDS, SEGREGATED FUNDS, EQUITIES, FIXED-INCOME PRODUCTS, AND INSURANCE.

Calgary Olympic Development Association

irst established in 1954, the Calgary Olympic Development Association (CODA) participated in three unsuccessful bids to host the Olympic Winter Games before winning the right for Calgary to host the 1988 Games. When Olympic Organization Committee (OOC) '88 was created in 1981 to manage the Games, CODA was restructured to manage their legacy. CODA's mandate was to ensure that there would be continuing use of the Olympic facilities for years to come. 🍁

Between 1982 and 1988, the association negotiated long-term amateur sport benefits from Pengrowth Saddledome, and ensured that the University of Calgary's Olympic Oval and the Canmore Nordic Centre would also be available to future athletes. After the Games, the Legacy Fund was established to help subsidize the operation of facilities so athletes could use them at nominal cost.

This foresight has paid off. Calgary is the only Winter Olympics city to continue to operate all its venues—many of them 365 days a year—for the training and competition of Canadian and international athletes. With an annual budget of about $20 million,

CALGARY OLYMPIC DEVELOPMENT ASSOCIATION (CODA) PRESIDENT JOHN MILLS SAYS, "CODA'S VISION IS TO BE AN INTERNATIONALLY RECOGNIZED LEADER IN THE DEVELOPMENT OF OLYMPIC WINTER SPORT ATHLETES, AND A KEY PARTNER IN ENHANCING CANADA'S BEST EVER PERFORMANCE AT THE GAMES."

half provided by the Legacy Fund and half from operating revenues at Canada Olympic Park, CODA hosts numerous world championships and world cups at each Olympic venue. In addition, the association provides more than $2 million in annual contributions to Canada's Olympic winter sports organizations.

Facilities Still Going Strong

anada Olympic Park, on the TransCanada Highway at the western edge of the city, is perhaps the most visible legacy of the 1988 Games to visitors and Calgarians alike.

Freestyle skiing, bobsleigh, luge, and ski jumping events took place at this venue.

The park has evolved into a year-round sport and tourist attraction, hosting more than half a million visitors each year. In addition to operating one of the largest ski schools in western Canada, Canada Olympic Park also maintains the largest Olympic Hall of Fame and Museum in North America, as well as offering unique programs that include summer sports camps and public bobsleigh and luge rides.

The Olympic Oval at the University of Calgary is another well-used venue. Canada Olympic Park and the university are partners

in financing and operating the oval. Comprising 26,000 square metres, the Olympic Oval was the first indoor speed skating oval in North America to offer ice in both summer and winter seasons.

"The oval is the fastest ice in the world, as is evidenced by its 24 official records in long track speed skating," says CODA President John Mills.

A national training centre for cross-country and biathlon teams, the Canmore Nordic Centre is complemented by a summer training facility on the Haig Glacier from July through October each year, as well as the $1.8 million Bill Warren Training Centre, which provides much-needed services for high-performance athletes.

The Next Legacy

CODA's vision is to be an internationally recognized leader in the development of Olympic winter sport athletes, and a key partner in enhancing Canada's best ever performance at the Games," says Mills.

Under its new planning process, called the Next Legacy, CODA's board of directors has identified a number of strategic policies to develop a full complement of winter sports training and competition facilities. The first step in the implementation of these strategies involves the construction of an indoor artificial ice start facility, for bobsleigh, luge, and skeleton competitors.

Other strategies involve the goal of bringing more world cup and world championship competitions to Calgary and the Bow Valley Corridor. CODA was a partner in the committee that won the rights to host the 2005 Goodwill Winter Games in Calgary and Alberta.

CODA has also partnered in establishing the National Sports Centre in Calgary. The centre works with athletes and coaches to ensure a positive and balanced approach to sport, assisting more than 350 nationally carded athletes achieve their performance goals, as well as helping many provincial-level athletes and coaches. Through the National Coaching Institute, provincial-level coaches learn new training techniques from high-performance coaches, while the Sport

Science Support Group provides information on training methods.

In another partnership with the Calgary Board of Education, CODA has established the National Sports School at William Aberhart High School. This program helps student athletes—hockey players and alpine skiers, for example—achieve both their educational and their sport goals. The school operates year-round to accommodate training and competition schedules.

"CODA is becoming the administrative hub of national winter sports, as more sports organizations relocate to the Calgary area," says Mills. "Some sports headquartered here include hockey, alpine and cross-country skiing, snow-boarding, ski jumping, luge, Nordic combined, and bobsleigh."

It's clear that these efforts will pay off—for Calgarians as well as for the rest of Canada—in the years to come, as CODA achieves its vision to support the complete development of Canadian Olympic winter athletes through facilities, training, funding, event organization, education, and sport delivery systems.

As Canada's largest private funder of winter sports development, CODA is committed to creating a brighter future for Canada's winter athletes, from the grass roots level to the country's Olympic best.

Global Television Network

The first television station to hit Calgary's airwaves in 1954, Calgary 7 has now become a key member of the Global Television Network, and is helping fulfil a long-time dream of Canwest Global owner Israel "Izzy" H. Asper. That ambitious dream is to become Canada's third major national network from coast to coast. In addition to the Canadian network, Global also has a strong presence in Australia, New Zealand, and Ireland. ❦

"We provide the best in entertainment and information programming with both Canadian and foreign content," says Jim Rusnak, President of Global TV Alberta. "Calgary 7 always had a strong local focus, but we're now part of a major network and have a much stronger international connection. Our coverage of international news has been further strengthened, and we expect to share high-quality programming or co-produce programs with other stations all over the world."

FROM LIVE BLACK AND WHITE, TO COLOUR FILM, TO VIDEOTAPE, SATELLITES, AND NOW DIGITAL TECHNOLOGY, GLOBAL TELEVISION HAS PIONEERED AND PERFECTED THE ENTERTAINMENT MEDIUM THAT HAS GROWN TO BECOME A HOUSEHOLD STAPLE.

Evolving Image

Global Television has had experience in shaping and reshaping its image through the years in response to changing times and the needs in the marketplace. The network's promotions and on-air look have always been innovative and leading edge.

Starting out as CBC affiliate CHCT, the television station was the first to bring this exciting new medium into people's homes. Hundreds of Calgarians flocked to the station's transmitter site seven miles west of the city limits to watch the engineers raise the first antenna. The demand for TV sets was so great that dealers had trouble filling orders.

The station evolved into The Rockin' Deuce in 1961. In 1966, the first colour pictures went on the air, and in 1967 the station was taken over by Selkirk Holdings. The station changed its call letters and began identifying itself as CFAC in 1971.

By the 1970s, Calgary Television had acquired its own colour studio cameras at

an investment of $180,000 each, and marvelled in the discovery of videotape. In 1975, the station severed its ties with CBC and became known as 2&7. Five years later, when Calgary won a National Hockey League franchise, the station acquired its first contract of many to televise Calgary Flames hockey games.

In the 1980s, the broadcasting industry launched into satellite technology. Sound and picture were transferred nearly instantaneously from anywhere in the world. Computers also burst on the scene, and further increased the speed and accuracy of television production and delivery.

In 1988, Calgary's only independent station was sold to Maclean Hunter, who, a few months later, sold the station to Western International Communications. In that same year, 2&7 Panda pins were a big hit when Calgary hosted the XV Winter Olympic Games. In 1993, the station freshened up its look to become Calgary 7, CICT (Independent Calgary Television), and went live on location with its first broadcast from a Rover microwave truck.

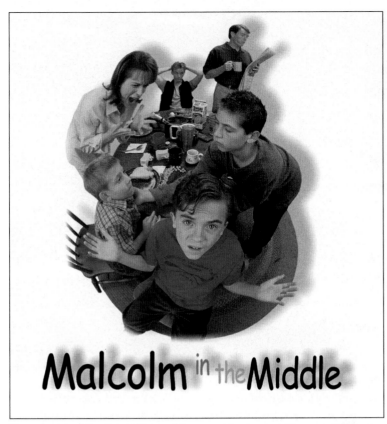

Malcolm in the Middle

WiLL & GRACe

The station joined the Global TV Network in the summer of 2000.

Global's Got It

The network's slogan, "Global's got it," rings very true as the station airs more top 10 shows than any other TV station in the southern Alberta market. Some of those shows include *Friends, The Simpsons, Frasier, The X-Files, Touched by an Angel, Dharma and Greg, Nash Bridges, Survivor, Will and Grace,* and *The Practice.* Global viewers are mostly adults ages 18 to 49 and women ages 25 to 54, the demographic groups that most advertisers want to reach.

"We've never been shy in taking risks, and we try to be ahead of the pack. We've always been that way," says Rusnak. "Now we're part of a great organization with that very same culture."

Throughout the years, the station has been recognized with numerous awards and honours from industry associations for its programming and its innovative marketing approach. Global Television has inspired audience loyalty by providing a mix of top-quality entertainment, with something for every viewer's taste.

In addition to providing morning, evening, and late night news and entertainment for southern Alberta viewers, Global Television produces a variety of special programming. For example, the station's Tony Tighe has been exposing scams, rip-offs, and consumer alerts for more than a decade as the city's consumer reporting expert. Tighe provides consumer information on air and has his research available on the station's Web site.

The *Global News Morning Edition* is Calgary's number one television morning show, with more than twice the number of

GLOBAL TELEVISION HAS INSPIRED AUDIENCE LOYALTY BY PROVIDING A MIX OF TOP-QUALITY ENTERTAINMENT, WITH SOMETHING FOR EVERY VIEWER'S TASTE.

GLOBAL TELEVISION HAS HAD EXPERIENCE IN SHAPING AND RESHAPING ITS IMAGE THROUGH THE YEARS IN RESPONSE TO CHANGING TIMES AND THE NEEDS IN THE MARKETPLACE.

viewers as any other station. The show offers everything viewers need to know to start their day with the latest in news, weather, and traffic. Regular features include a job line, travel tips, Adopt A Pet, Zoo News, New On Video, pet tips, parenting teens, Saturday chef, What's It Worth, Fashion 911, and home hints.

Global operates one of the leading production houses in the city, complete with the latest technology and full post-production facilities. In addition to producing its own promotions and TV commercials, as well as those for other Global stations, Global Television rents its facilities to others in the community. The facilities are equipped with award-winning writer/producers and directors; Super-16mm film and Beta-SP video production; lighting direction; media-100 digital editing with broadcast output; full-facility, one-inch linear editing; 2D/3D graphic design; set design; and carpentry services. There is also a mobile division—a production house on wheels—that is often used to cover sporting events such as World Cup skiing and NHL hockey.

Community Involvement

Global has always been dedicated to community involvement. Giving back has been part of the station's history. "We're the oldest station in the market, and many of our relationships with local organizations have been going on for decades," says Jeff Eisler, director of creative services for Global Television in Alberta.

The station offers free publicity for non-profit groups on a daily basis. Local events, issues, and people are also profiled on the *Global News Morning Edition*, and even more city happenings are featured on the evening news.

The Spirit of Calgary sponsors and participates in more than 100 community events each year. In many cases, the station has been the original sponsor since the event first took place. Global has sponsored the Children's Miracle Network Telethon to raise millions of dollars annually to support the Alberta Children's Hospital. The proceeds from the sale of the 2&7 Panda pins during the pin-trading mania of the 1988 Olympics

were also donated to the hospital.

In addition, the station is the official entertainment sponsor for the Calgary Exhibition and Stampede, presenting all entertainment on Stampede Park during the fun-filled 10 days of Stampede. The station also helps sponsor Zoogala, the official annual fund-raising event for the Calgary Zoo, as well as the annual Calgary Corporate Challenge.

In addition to ongoing annual sponsorships, Global supports many other one-time programs and activities. The station promoted Forever Green Calgary, an urban forestry program involving community tree planting; care and maintenance education; and fundraising to purchase, plant, and maintain new trees. The trees were planted in high-priority locations by volunteers.

Global also promoted a Shaw Millennium Park fundraiser, which provided an opportunity for Calgarians to make their Mark in the Park at Calgary's first skateboarding park near the Mewata Stadium.

Sometimes the station will initiate and organize worthy events on its own. Of note, in 1992 when the city's economy took a nose-

dive and thousands of Calgarians suffered layoffs, the station took it upon itself to try to get people back to work. By pulling together resources from the federal government employment offices, local career counselling groups, and potential employers, Global co-ordinated and produced three prime-time special jobathons called "Working Together." Hundreds of Calgarians were employed as a result of these efforts.

Low Turnover

The station has forged long-term relationships with its employees, and has one of the lowest turnover rates in the business. "Employees don't leave," notes Rusnak. "They just have too much fun working here."

No one exemplifies that commitment better than Ed Whalen, one of the most well-known Global Television personalities. Whalen began his affiliation with the station in 1955, almost from the time it first went on the air. He spent almost 25 years as news and sports director, starting out as a one-man department. In 1979, Whalen formed his own company, and went on contract to the station with a mandate to broadcast the supper-hour sports and Flames hockey games.

A local legend and a great city advocate, Whalen is perhaps most famous—at least to the rest of the world—for his years with *Stampede Wrestling*. "I was the only news director in the world with a wrestling show on the side," Whalen says. "That was great comic relief in my life." It was the end of an era for both Calgary and Whalen when *Stampede Wrestling* stopped production in 1988.

"Today we're faced with a growing number of more sophisticated, more sceptical viewers," notes Rusnak. "Many of them are getting tired of neatly packaged programming; the demand for uncut, unrehearsed television is on the rise. So we now find ourselves on the cutting edge of the information highway, but this time we're delivering a product not unlike that which first hit the airwaves in 1954. Our challenge then is to continue to flourish with each change, fostering technological and creative innovation while catering to the needs of our viewers."

As for the future, the station expects to expand now that it is part of a bigger network. "We'll be exploring new media and looking for opportunities to work with our network partners," says Rusnak.

From live black and white, to colour film, to videotape, satellites, and now digital technology, Global Television has pioneered and perfected the entertainment medium that has grown to become a household staple. Through name changes, programming changes, and sweeping technological changes, one thing has remained constant: the station's pride and commitment to the community—its undying support of the spirit of Calgary.

THE STATION HAS FORGED LONG-TERM RELATIONSHIPS WITH ITS EMPLOYEES, AND HAS ONE OF THE LOWEST TURNOVER RATES IN THE BUSINESS. "EMPLOYEES DON'T LEAVE," NOTES JIM RUSNAK, PRESIDENT OF GLOBAL TV ALBERTA. "THEY JUST HAVE TOO MUCH FUN WORKING HERE."

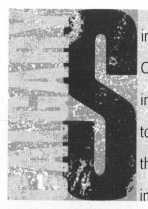

ince 1955, when it took over the operations of Middleton & Tate, Marsh Canada, Limited has been providing comprehensive and innovative risk and insurance services to its Calgary clients. The company's history dates back to the late 1800s, when two pioneers began a tradition of innovation in the fledgling industry. ❦ Henry Marsh first introduced the concept of an insurance broker acting as a buyer representing the client, rather than as a

seller of insurance, in 1897. He also pioneered the concept of risk management a few years later by setting forth his ideas on a comprehensive risk management plan for U.S. Steel. In the meantime, Don McLennan was establishing a standard for thorough research in establishing risk, spending 30 consecutive nights traveling coast to coast to inspect the operations of two U.S. railroad lines.

It was inevitable that the two men's paths would cross, and in 1905, they formed the world's largest insurance agency, with annual premiums of $3 million. Through the years, the company has expanded, and by 1999, Marsh & McLennan Companies, Inc. (MMC) had grown to become a global professional services firm with more than 50,000 employees providing services to corporate, institutional, and individual clients in more than 100 countries.

MMC is the parent of three businesses: Marsh, the world's leading risk and insurance services firm; Putnam, one of the largest investment management companies in the United States; and Mercer, a major global provider of corporate consulting services.

Each firm has prospered based on a commitment to serve the interests of clients and the ability to anticipate clients' needs, as well as the ability to adapt services and capabilities accordingly.

Calgary Office

arsh Canada's Calgary office offers a full range of insurance services, including aviation, personal client services, risk consulting, risk management, and insurance brokerage with a staff of some 150 available to assist with these services.

Marsh has steadily built its business beyond insurance brokering—where it remains the world leader—to encompass a full range of services to identify, quantify, mitigate, transfer, and finance risk. A critical influence on the profitability and financial strength of any organization is the total cost of risk. Marsh helps clients manage their risks to strengthen their balance sheets and benefit their bottom line.

Marsh's client services include risk consulting—helping clients valuate their risk exposures and optimize their risk

retentions—as well as an ever widening range of risk transfer and financing techniques. Marsh has unrivalled knowledge of the resources of worldwide insurance markets—and the technology to access them swiftly.

New Opportunities in Globalization

lobalization is one factor that seriously affects the risk management and insurance industry as companies conduct business outside of their home countries. Deregulation and the liberalization of markets are creating new opportunities in many areas as e-commerce continues to boom. All of these trends are increasing risk.

"The growing complexity of the business world creates new and expanded risks," notes Peter Redmond, Managing Director, Western Regional Manager. "So our role as advisers and providers of solutions involving risk is becoming even more valuable."

Marsh has developed its Risk Solutions Network to meet the ever increasing needs of clients' emerging risks; rogue/unauthorized trading, tax opinion guarantee protection, letter-of-credit replacement vehicles, litigation

cost caps, power price protection, strategic risk assessments, and more. As well, a network of worldwide industry focus professionals functions nationally through the company's newly launched Knowledge Management System.

An example of Marsh at work is a risk transfer vehicle for companies engaged in business-to-business e-commerce. Marsh developed the product while consulting with a growing dot-com that brokers electricity and natural gas on its Web site. The client's revenue growth was being constrained due to suppliers' and customers' concerns about transaction risks. Suppliers were concerned that buyers might default on their purchases, while buyers were concerned that suppliers might not deliver the agreed-upon energy. The client lacked the resources to provide the financial security required by customers and suppliers. Marsh secured a counterparty credit insurance program that protects suppliers when energy buyers fail to pay. Marsh is also creating an expanded program to cover the buyer's risk that a supplier may default on delivery of energy.

Strong Growth

With a compound annual growth rate of 15 percent in the past 15 years, parent company MMC has achieved results in a world where change has proved to be the company's ally.

"We've extended the range of our professional services," says Redmond. "We've grown internally and added new focus to enhance our capability to solve clients' increasingly complex problems." Staffing now includes some of the most sought after talent available with varying backgrounds such as MBAs, accountants, and traders, as well as insurance professionals, to match the company's solution-driven business.

MMC and Marsh Canada have withstood the test of time by producing work for clients that meets the highest standards during periods of challenging and rapidly changing business conditions. Looking ahead, there are exciting opportunities for continued growth of the business.

1886 Buffalo Café

Not many buildings in Calgary can lay claim to being more than 100 years old, but when visitors first see the 1886 Buffalo Café, they sense right away that this charming restaurant is infused with history. The small building, which dates back to 1886, has been designated an historical building. It was that year that entrepreneur and pioneer Isaac Kerr and General Manager P.A. "Pete" Prince saw the potential for a viable lumber industry,

and established the Eau Claire Lumber Company of Calgary. At its peak, the company employed more than 150 workers, providing significant economic benefit to Calgary, a brand-new frontier town. Prince's Island is named after P.A. Prince.

Current visitors can spend time in the pictorial museum in the café building's basement, where the early days are commemorated with dozens of historical photos. Upstairs, still visible from the dining room, is the vault where townspeople brought their valuables for safekeeping, as it was the only vault in Calgary at that time. Worn floorboards still stand testament to the thousands of transactions that took place when the building housed the lumber business. On the walls can be seen a collection of buffalo heads, icon to an era long gone.

With a seating capacity of 60, the building has housed a restaurant since 1959, when a legendary one-armed cook used to feed bus drivers from the nearby bus barns, according to current owner Wayne Hemming, who purchased the operation in 1977, at a time when the Eau Claire area was still totally undeveloped.

"I was in the right place at the right time," Hemming says. "The rent was about

$60 a month, and I lived in the basement. Sometimes a customer would order something, and I would have to jump in my car to make a trip to Safeway."

From the beginning, Hemming's restaurant offered a breakfast menu only, with hash browns as its main claim to fame.

Over the years, the menu has not changed significantly. The same cannot be said about the restaurant's clientele, however. In the early years, the restaurant was popular with an eclectic cross section of colourful characters—from bad guys and bikers to judges.

As the Eau Claire area began to be developed, the restaurant's clientele began to develop as well. Business people and tourists started to form a larger portion of the restaurant's patrons, as well as members of the film industry and major sports teams.

1886 is one of a small handful of restaurants to pass the 20-year mark in Calgary. Then, as now, information about the restaurant travelled by word of mouth; there has been no commercial advertising. Hotels steer visitors to the restaurant, and they come away thinking they've seen a very special part of Calgary.

Owner-operators Hemming and Blaise McNeill have been asked many times why 1886 Buffalo Café does not open for the evenings, but the current set-up suits them fine. The restaurant's busiest time is before other restaurants are open. Hemming and McNeill know a good thing—and they're not willing to tinker with success.

THE 1886 BUFFALO CAFÉ, ONE OF A SMALL HANDFUL OF RESTAURANTS TO PASS THE 20-YEAR MARK IN CALGARY, IS OWNED AND OPERATED BY WAYNE HEMMING AND BLAISE MCNEILL.

The evening of September 9, 1960, brought H. Gordon Love's dream to a reality. It was then that CFCN Television went on the air for the first time. Years of hard work and dedication followed, turning Love's dream into the most popular television station in Calgary. The legacy of innovative ideas about news, entertainment, and community involvement continues today as the station broadcasts across southern Alberta. ❧ Since CFCN's first moment on the air, the station

has been visionary. As an owned and operated affiliate of the CTV Network, CFCN created a number of firsts in Canadian television, including being the first to produce a Canadian Football League game from the prairies for CTV, and instituting instant replay in western Canada. CFCN also brought Crime Stoppers to Calgary and initiated Child Find on television.

Responding to the growing demand for consumer and medical news, CFCN was one of the first newsrooms in Canada to create a consumer beat known as Consumer Watch and a medical segment called Health Watch.

"The Royal Canadian Mounted Police, the City of Calgary, and the Better Business Bureau routinely refer complainants to our newsroom," says Patricia McDougall, Vice President and General Manager of the station. "They claim CFCN can have more impact and create more positive change than they can. Health Watch has had similar credibility in the medical community."

News Leader

Over the last decade, CFCN's newscasts have been rated number one in southern Alberta. With more weekday viewers than all its competitors combined, *CFCN News* has set itself apart and is Calgary's news leader. This tradition carries over on weekends, where the *Sunday News* at 6 p.m. has triple the viewers of the nearest competitor.

"We're also renowned for our on-air talent," says McDougall. "Our senior news anchor/producer Darrel Janz has been

with CFCN for more than 25 years and is very active within the community. He and co-anchor/producer Barb Higgins consistently win newspaper and radio polls as the most recognizable and trusted personalities in the city."

Calgarians have also looked to CFCN for outstanding entertainment. From early programs such as the *Calgary Safety Round Up Show*, to children's programming like the famous *Buck Shot Show*, Calgarians have invited CFCN into their living rooms. *Law & Order*, *ER*, and *The West Wing* are just some of the powerhouse dramas found on the current program schedule. Major entertainment awards shows such as the Oscars, the Emmys, the Grammys, and the Golden Globe Awards can also be seen on CFCN.

CFCN does much more than inform and entertain. Through the past 40 years, CFCN

has held community involvement as a central philosophy. Involved in a host of charity fundraisers, CFCN continues to support and promote numerous non-profit organizations, including the Canadian Breast Cancer Foundation, Alberta Children's Hospital Foundation, Calgary Native Friendship Centre, Junior Achievement, and Volunteer Calgary.

The future looks bright for CFCN. In 2000 Bell Canada Enterprises acquired CTV in a $2.3 billion transaction. Thus, Canada's largest telecommunications company joined hands with the country's largest private broadcaster, resulting in exciting new content and services for Canadians. Committed as ever to excellence in news and programming, CFCN endeavors to improve the quality of life in Calgary through community involvement and to leave a lasting legacy for the Canadian broadcasting system.

THE NEWSCASTS OF CFCN TELEVISION HAVE BEEN RATED NUMBER ONE IN SOUTHERN ALBERTA FOR MORE THAN A DECADE.

FROM SKYWATCH WEATHER TO ENTERTAINMENT FOR WEEKDAY VIEWERS AND EVEN COMMUNITY INVOLVEMENT, CFCN SETS THE STANDARD FOR BROADCAST EXCELLENCE.

Mantei's Transport Ltd.

hen 26-year-old Erwin Mantei immigrated to Calgary from Germany in 1956 with his wife and two small children, he did so with a firm belief that hard work and perseverance would lead to opportunity and success. Within three short years, he had purchased a flatbed hauling truck and had begun to transport a variety of goods. ❧ From this single truck, Mantei's Transport Ltd. has become the fourth-largest hauler of refined

petroleum products in Alberta, with 58 trucks, 50 tank trailers, 21 van trailers, more than 100 employees, and revenues that have doubled in the last decade. The torch of entrepreneurship has been transferred to the next generation—Erwin's four children: Jurgen, Ron, Monica, and Armin.

Hard Work and Strategic Decisions

The path to success involved some key decisions by Erwin Mantei. After hauling various products with his truck for a few years, he decided to focus on bulk petroleum liquids, which provided a stable market, long-term contracts, and fewer—but more sizable—customers. Mantei was fortunate to become a subcontractor with H.M. Trimble & Sons—the future Trimac.

"My dad decided to specialize in bulk petroleum liquids because there were more

opportunities to build relationships with customers," says Jurgen Mantei, now president of the company. "You can be more proactive about developing relationships, since these types of customers value service over cost."

A major milestone in the history of Mantei's came in 1969, when Erwin Mantei secured a long-term contract with Gibson Petroleum. With a staff of more than 15—mostly drivers—the company opened an

office with Mantei assuming the role of mechanic, driver, dispatcher, accountant, office manager, president, and just about any other duty required for the business to operate.

In 1978, Mantei sold his flatbed trucks and purchased PJK Services, the dedicated refined products carrier for Shell Oil, beginning a relationship with Shell that is still going strong today. During that same period, Mantei's children assumed various responsibilities in the company.

By 1984, their involvement was solidified through the creation of a board of directors, with all four children sitting on the board. From the 1980s to the mid-1990s, Mantei's experienced a period of incredible growth, with expansion into both British Columbia and the United States.

Yet at the same time, there were also challenges. As the oil and gas industry underwent a period of consolidation, involving a number of mergers and acquisitions, so too did the trucking industry. Mantei's was one of the few survivors, largely due to the company's growing reputation as a safe and reliable carrier.

In 1997, Petro-Canada, a major customer, transferred its inventory management of gasoline at service stations to Mantei's. Mantei's was no longer simply a carrier, but had to develop a sophisticated inventory management system, and today manages the inventory of more than 80 gas stations.

A Unique Culture

While many companies espouse certain traits and values, it is obvious that the management of Mantei's believes actions speak louder than words. "We thought about developing a comprehensive mission statement in the early 1990s, but our culture is really deeper than a set of words can describe," says Jurgen Mantei.

Attracting and keeping the best drivers has been part of that culture. "Trucking tends to be a high turnover industry," notes Jurgen Mantei. "We were the first in the industry to pay drivers by the hour, rather than per load or per kilometre. There are also bonus and incentive programs for the drivers, as well as deferred profit sharing. We have an annual awards banquet where our drivers are recognized for their years of service, their safety record, and even for acting as a Good Samaritan on the road."

At Mantei's, safety is an important focus in its own right. Safety issues are minimized with new, more reliable equipment. The majority of Mantei's trucks are fewer than four years old. All trucks are equipped with onboard computers that monitor driver performance and hours worked. Drivers receive

ERWIN MANTEI'S FOUR CHILDREN—(FROM LEFT) RON, ARMIN, MONICA, AND JURGEN—HAVE ASSUMED VARIOUS RESPONSIBILITES WITHIN THE COMPANY.

regular safety training and annual retraining to keep their skills sharp. The company is also a participant in the Partners in Compliance (PIC) program, an industry-government partnership to encourage self-reporting of rule violations.

"To be a PIC carrier, you must be audited and certified, and only a very small percentage of trucking companies in Alberta qualify for this program," says Jurgen Mantei. With significant in-house expertise, Mantei's

has also developed a reputation for its ability to react in emergency situations, whether cleaning up a fuel spill or helping out other carriers in distress.

And now, the children of the four Mantei siblings are taking on roles in the business. With the third generation of the family becoming involved, Mantei's is poised to grow for decades to come. But it's clear that no one will forget how Erwin Mantei's dedication and hard work built a successful business.

Trimac Corporation

Trimac Corporation traces its roots back to Saskatchewan in the Dirty Thirties, when Scottish immigrant and farmer Jack McCaig first established a trucking company. His motivation came from seeing his 98-pound mother spill 100-pound cans of milk that she had hauled by horse and buggy to the railway station, but couldn't lift onto the platform. ☀ By 1932, McCaig had sold the milk run and had begun moving oil company warehouses from

railroad-owned land to new sites. In 1945, McCaig and partner Al Cameron launched Maccam Transport, marking the official beginning of Trimac. A new holding company was formed in 1960 and named Trimac Limited for the three McCaig sons—Bud, Roger, and Maurice—all of whom had joined the business at an early age.

The company expanded into Alberta with the purchase of Calgary-based H.M. Trimble & Sons in 1960. "By the mid-1960s, we saw our role in the transportation business as more broad-based," says Bud McCaig. "There were no national bulk carriers at that time, and we could see great opportunity for growth. Anything that could be poured or shoveled or scooped could be hauled in tank-type vehicles." Trimac continued to expand its trucking operations across Canada, and in 1980, it moved into the U.S. market with the purchase of Liquid Transporters of Louisville, Kentucky.

TRIMAC CORPORATION, FOUNDED IN 1945 BY JACK MCCAIG AND AL CAMERON, SPECIALIZES IN BULK TRUCKING AND LOGISTICS.

A Family Tradition

In 1994, carrying on the family tradition, Jeff McCaig, son of Bud McCaig, took over as the president of the company; Bud McCaig remains as the chairman of the company's board of directors. Jeff McCaig has taken the steps needed to move Trimac into the new millennium.

In response to changes in the capital markets, the company has focused on its core business of bulk trucking and logistics. The purchase of Houston-based DSI Transports in late 1999 increased bulk trucking revenues 50 percent, and extended the company's reach throughout North America through a network of facilities in 150 locations. "NAFTA has opened doors for us, and while trucking is considered a mature industry in the United States and Canada, there are still untapped markets in cross-border trucking with Mexico," notes Jeff McCaig.

The decision to move into the booming logistics field is a natural outgrowth of the company's core business. "We're a service industry, and we must continue to add

increased value to our customers," says Jeff McCaig. "The transportation component of the supply chain provides opportunities for our customers to improve their efficiency. We have the expertise to help them achieve that competitive edge."

Throughout the years, Trimac has prided itself on a reputation for innovation. The company was one of the first bulk haulers in North America to initiate two-way hauling with trailers that could carry both liquids and dry bulk. Innovation continues, with the implementation of customized, state-of-the-art information technology systems allowing computerized dispatch and satellite communication with truck drivers.

Despite the extraordinary success of the company, one overriding essential fact remains. "My goal has always been to build a significant North American company based in western Canada," says Bud McCaig. And although Trimac is one of the largest bulk trucking companies in North America, McCaig's word has been good—Trimac continues to maintain its head office in Calgary.

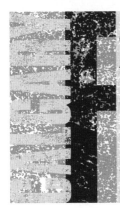

ounded in 1965 in a vacant showroom of a car dealership to help disadvantaged adults upgrade their education, Bow Valley College (BVC) has since come a long way. Today, BVC is a post-secondary educational institution serving more than 11,000 students each year in Calgary and throughout southern Alberta. With an emphasis on work force preparation and development, Bow Valley College offers credit programs on both a full- and a part-time basis.

"We're quite different from most other post-secondary institutions," says President Sharon Carry. "First of all, we take programs out of the college to where the learners are." The college's largest program area is in Academic Upgrading. English as a second language (ESL) training also comprises a significant portion of the offerings. Career training is the other main program area, with a focus on front-line employees. More than 20 career certificates are offered.

For example, the college runs programs at three correctional institutions and six reservations, as well as at work sites such as the 24-hour-a-day learning centre at Calgary's Transit Barns, where drivers coming off shift can hone their computer literacy and other skills. The college even seeks out learners with no fixed address. "We're currently participating on a task force to reach out to street youth, by offering learning centres where they hang out," says Carry.

and incorporated into the Colleges Act. The name change to Bow Valley College reflects the institution's mandate to serve southern Alberta, with additional campuses at Airdrie, Canmore, and Strathmore, as well as offerings through local colleges in Red Deer, Lethbridge, and Medicine Hat. The college also partners to offer programs in Drumheller, Stettler, Claresholm, Cardston, Fort Macleod, Pincher Creek, and Blairmore.

But truly, the college's impact has spread far beyond Alberta's borders. Operating the country's largest ESL centre after Toronto and Vancouver, Bow Valley has developed programs for China, Guyana, and South Africa. In what is the longest-standing contractual arrangement between China and Canada, Bow Valley has provided ESL training to engineers and technicians in Calgary's twin city, Daqing, since 1983. The college also attracts increasing numbers of international students to its ESL programs.

a full program with new curriculum," says Carry. "The only catch was they needed to have it in place by Saturday. For other post-secondary institutions, that time frame would have been impossible—they would need two years to develop the curriculum. But we have an absolute can-do attitude without a lot of bureaucracy, so we were able to pull it off."

The college also partners with clients who are recruiting new employees by providing assessment services to determine applicants' skills. "We help companies across Canada develop recruitment and training programs," says Carry. "We have effective tools to test for essential workplace skills, such as literacy and numeracy."

Being fast, focused, and flexible has allowed Bow Valley College to carve out a niche in the changing world of learning, and will help the college succeed in the years to come.

BOW VALLEY COLLEGE, A POST-SECONDARY EDUCATIONAL INSTITUTION SERVING MORE THAN 11,000 STUDENTS EACH YEAR, FOCUSES ON WORK FORCE PREPARATION AND DEVELOPMENT, AND OFFERS CREDIT PROGRAMS ON BOTH A FULL- AND A PART-TIME BASIS.

For Alberta and Beyond

irst known as the Alberta Vocational Centre, BVC was founded in 1965 by the Alberta government. In 1998, the college was divested by the government, becoming board governed

A Customized Curriculum

ow Valley customizes a number of its programs in collaboration with industry clients who want training courses for their staff. "One time we had a client call on a Tuesday, requesting

Top Notch Construction Ltd.

When Alex Lockton bought his first tractor at age 17 in 1966, little did he imagine that almost 40 years later he would be heading up a construction company with more than 150 employees and 165 pieces of construction equipment. With an annual production volume of $16 million to $20 million, Top Notch Construction Ltd. does construction work for dams, canals, highways, subdivisions, and industrial sites in Calgary and southern Alberta.

Lockton's hard work started showing results right away. By 1972, he and his wife, Gayle, a major contributor to the business, were living in a small home in Calgary, as the company began to build roads for the county of Rockyview. In 1980, Lockton established Top Notch Aggregate Ltd., a gravel-washing and -crushing business. A major break came in 1981 with the construction company's first large project, a water reservoir at Bow Island.

Large projects soon became the norm for Top Notch. Between 1985 and 1990, the company worked on the Highway 22 construction, St. Mary's Irrigation District's canals, Highway 22X, and the Oldman River Dam, one of Canada's largest earthwork projects—collectively worth more than $27 million in billings.

Ahead of Schedule

Clients continue to seek out Top Notch because the company delivers. A more recent project—building an intermodal site for the Canadian Pacific Railway—was completed seven months ahead of schedule. "We've never been behind," says Lockton. "We put more workers on and work seven days a week to make sure we meet our deadlines."

Top Notch completes its projects on time, without any reduction in quality. It is common in the construction business to provide maintenance services for one year, but the quality of Top Notch's work is so high that the company has never had to carry out any maintenance.

Top Notch's reputation for good, quality work resulted in the company's being awarded the only two design-build projects in southern Alberta in 1999. Top Notch beat out international as well as local competitors to construct a waste water disposal system for a new McCain's potato processing plant near Coaldale. The company acted as general contractor and earthmover—putting together a team of engineers and building, underground, mechanical, and electrical subcontractors to develop a plan that would meet McCain's needs.

The company's other design-build project in Alberta in 1999 involved the construction of 96th Avenue, the new Calgary Airport access road off Deerfoot Trail.

"When we were building the detour, we made sure three lanes were always open in each direction, so traffic wouldn't slow down," says Lockton.

The Right Tools

In addition to being on time and on budget, Top Notch has every type of earth-moving equipment to do any kind of construction work. Every year, a few more pieces are added to the inventory. With a shop and some 20 mechanics, the company is able to buy used equipment at lower cost and refurbish it. "We also build all of our own attachments, if we need something special to complete a job," says Lockton.

Top Notch's mechanical ability has helped the company stay ahead of the industry

WITH AN ANNUAL PRODUCTION VOLUME OF $16 MILLION TO $20 MILLION, TOP NOTCH CONSTRUCTION LTD. DOES CONSTRUCTION WORK FOR DAMS, CANALS, HIGHWAYS, SUBDIVISIONS, AND INDUSTRIAL SITES IN CALGARY AND SOUTHERN ALBERTA.

▲ KAUTZ

technically. For example, the firm was one of the first construction companies to use spinning lasers for grade control, and Top Notch's robotic controls have allowed surveying activities to be carried out by a single worker rather than two.

The company's seasoned management team is noted throughout the industry for its integrity and honesty, as well as being easy to work with. Eight Top Notch employees have received Gold Seal certification through the Canadian Construction Association.

"For every project we try to determine the most efficient, economical way to get it done without sacrificing quality," says Lockton. "We often offer suggestions to engineering companies to improve a design, and even consult with them before they submit a proposal."

▲ KAUTZ

An Excellent Safety Record

Another benefit Top Notch brings to the table is its excellent safety record. Construction work on highways and in other public places can be quite dangerous, but no Top Notch worker has ever had a serious injury.

"The worst accident we've had is a broken finger," says Lockton. "I tease my guys that they get hurt more playing than working."

Top Notch has received a certificate of recognition from the Partnerships in Health and Safety Program of the Alberta Construction Safety Association for its implementation of a workplace health and safety management system.

The company also has an environmental policy requiring that equipment be maintained in a clean and serviceable condition, fuel and oil leaks be repaired promptly,

▲ KAUTZ

oil evacuation systems be used wherever possible, shop facilities be kept clean, and work in stream beds and other sensitive areas be carried out within authorized time periods and with due regard for the environment.

Although Lockton misses the assistance of Gayle, who died in 2000, two sons-in-law

work in the business now and his daughters are directors of the company. "I believe we're well respected by the competition," Lockton says. "We sometimes go head to head, but we wish our competitors well and will support them if they need our help. Our goal is to do the best possible job—that's why our name is Top Notch."

CLIENTS CONTINUE TO SEEK OUT TOP NOTCH BECAUSE THE COMPANY DELIVERS. IT COMPLETES ITS PROJECTS ON TIME, WITHOUT ANY REDUCTION IN QUALITY.

University of Calgary

The University of Calgary—located on 123 hectares in the central northwest part of the city—is a thriving teaching and research-intensive university that has been quick to position itself in the new marketplace. As many post-secondary institutions are reviewing their mandate in light of recent techno-logical changes, the educational traditions of the past are being molded into new approaches to higher education. ☀ "We're a contemporary university that builds a spirit of discipline and inquiry while delivering a dynamic lifestyle and a quality learning experience," says Dr. Ron Bond, Vice-President, academic.

Innovative Options

With more than 30,000 students passing under its landmark arch every year, the university is breaking new ground in curriculum design and course delivery. A number of innovative options are available, such as interdisciplinary majors, cooperative education and internships, hands-on research opportunities, international study experiences, and theme schools in cooperation with affiliated institutions.

"We also make sure that students have lots of opportunities to interact—both face to face and electronically—with their professors and classmates," says Bond.

Research Orientation

Recognized as having the best law school by *Canadian Lawyer* magazine, the University of Calgary has also developed a worldwide reputation for quality research. The university is one of Canada's most research-intensive universities, involving hundreds of projects and more than $134 million in research funding annually. Sixteen faculties—from engineering to medicine to fine arts to social work—are actively involved in research.

Medical research is another important area of study, with many important breakthroughs. For example, in November 1998, cancer researcher Dr. Patrick Lee and his colleagues announced to the world that they had found a naturally occurring and harmless human virus that kills cancer cells in mice. While this news has brought hope to many cancer patients, hundreds of thousands of people in some 25 countries have already benefited from a unique water filter designed by a University of Calgary civil engineering professor.

International Aspect

Many employers are looking for graduates with international experience and second languages. The University of Calgary has more than 150 exchange programs with universities world-wide to broaden students' cultural and academic experiences.

"One of our most important roles is to be a place where cultures meet," says Bond. The university maintains strong international ties through hosting visiting professors, and through learning exchanges and international conferences. In addition, the Gorbachev Foundation, established in 1993 by Mikhail Gorbachev, is situated at the University of Calgary. The foundation is an international nonprofit organization funding public policy programs and projects, and facilitating the transfer of Canadian expertise overseas. Among other initiatives, the foundation funded a training program to teach Russian teachers about democracy, as well as a proposal for a comprehensive, efficient unemployment insurance program for Russia.

Calgary and education naturally go together. Of all of Canada's major cities, Calgary's population is the most educated. University of Calgary students are fortunate to enjoy the benefit of a world-class education along with a quality of living that is unsurpassed.

WITH MORE THAN 30,000 STUDENTS ATTENDING THE UNIVERSITY EACH YEAR, THE UNIVERSITY OF CALGARY IS A THRIVING TEACHING AND RESEARCH-INTENSIVE UNIVERSITY THAT HAS BEEN QUICK TO POSITION ITSELF IN THE NEW MARKETPLACE.

Young oil and gas companies often start off as private, family-owned businesses, but Sabre Energy Ltd. has stayed that way. Sabre has resisted the lure to sell out or go public since it was taken over by local oilman Jack Pirie in 1979. Noted Calgarian and Calgary Flames owner Harley Hotchkiss originally established the company in 1967 as Sabre Petroleums Ltd., and the firm changed hands in 1976 prior to Pirie's involvement. ◆ In the

1970s Jack Pirie was employed by Dome Petroleum, primarily to evaluate acquisition opportunities. When he left the company in 1978, he was familiar with Sabre and struck a deal with Dome whereby he obtained roughly half of the producing properties in Sabre's portfolio—those located in Alberta—and Dome purchased the other half. In addition, Sabre constructed a 1,000 metric ton-a-day nitrogen plant, and entered into a supply contract with Dome that provided the main source of revenues during Sabre's first few years under Pirie's stewardship. Sabre was producing 940 barrels of oil equivalent (BOE) daily of mostly natural gas in 1980, and by 1999 the company had acquired positions in more properties and was producing 2,800 BOE daily, at a ratio of two-thirds oil to one-third gas.

Family Business

Jack Pirie's son Neal Pirie, who came on board in 1991, also has a solid oil and gas background from working at Amoco, Bow Valley Industries, and Syncrude. Neal is now president and CEO of Sabre, while Jack, who is semiretired, is chairman of the board. Jack's daughter Kim Cook, a geologist by profession, is also involved with the company as manager of exploration and corporate affairs. And Jack's son Mark Pirie, who is involved in real estate in California, has also played a role at Sabre by providing the company with an opportunity to purchase and sell the Altius Centre, a major office building in downtown Calgary.

"Being private and family owned allows us more freedom," says Neal Pirie. "We continue to dabble in opportunities outside the oil and gas sector, such as our interest in a wind energy and power technology company. By diversifying, we reduce the impact of the cyclical nature of oil and gas, and can time our oil and gas purchases when the market is down."

Chairman Jack Pirie is proud that his children have joined him at Sabre. In addition to her duties as a geologist, Cook manages the Pirie Foundation, set up by Jack in 1993 to provide funding for causes close to his heart.

"I have strong feelings about education and how children are being taught, so the foundation supports private grade schools as well as post-secondary institutions," says Jack Pirie. "We also provide funding for think-tanks—such as the Fraser Institute—that share our public policy views."

Jack and his children also take pride in the company's 12 employees. "It's a close-knit group," says Neal Pirie. "Many of our employees have been here longer than I have."

In 22 years, Jack and his children have taken Sabre from being $39 million in debt to having a healthy cash surplus, equivalent to three times its annual cash flow. "We're definitely in a strong position to take advantage of new opportunities," says Pirie.

JACK PIRIE IS SABRE ENERGY LTD.'S CHAIRMAN OF THE BOARD, WHILE DAUGHTER KIM COOK IS MANAGER OF EXPLORATION AND CORPORATE AFFAIRS AND SON NEAL SERVES AS PRESIDENT AND CEO.

SABRE'S HEAD OFFICE STAFF FORM A CLOSE-KNIT GROUP.

Metso Automation

Enabling RealTime business is Metso Automation's primary focus, which helps explain how and why the company has evolved over the past decade from a traditional Supervisory Control and Data Acquisition (SCADA) supplier to a provider of RealTime information solutions. ♦ Metso Automation is a leading developer of RealTime automation and information management systems, remote monitoring and control solutions, and simulation products for the oil and gas, water and wastewater, and electric utility industries worldwide. The Calgary office of Metso Automation heads up the corporation's SCADA and RealTime information management operations unit, and is supported by regional offices in Houston, Baltimore, and Ankara, as well as sales offices in various locations around the globe.

Early Beginnings

The company's roots took hold in Calgary in 1969 as a privately held electronics, software, and communications company serving the local Alberta oil patch. During a series of Canadian mergers over the next 15 years, the firm established itself as a leading SCADA supplier to the U.S. market. In 1986, the company was acquired by Finnish paper industry giant Valmet Corporation, adding momentum for a successful expansion into the international marketplace.

During the late 1980s, the evolution of standards-based open systems architecture, combined with hardware and software technology advances, created the ideal environment for launching Metso Automation's OASyS (Open Architecture System) SCADA and information management system. The industry quickly embraced the significant advantages offered by OASyS, including its cross-platform capabilities and ease of integration with different networks and relational databases. As a result, the company captured and has since maintained the majority share of the North American oil and gas pipeline SCADA market.

"Our first OASyS sale was to Colonial Pipeline Company in the United States, which operates the world's longest common carrier refined products pipeline in the world," says Dave Jardine, division president. "Colonial's network extends over 8,500 kilometres from the Gulf of Mexico to New York Harbor, and carries more than 2 million barrels of product per day. This was a very significant contract for us—after that, the number of OASyS sales leapt almost exponentially."

With OASyS, the role of the traditional SCADA platform was expanded to include operations and business management functions, such as electronic flow measurement and volumetric revenue accounting for oil and gas pipelines. Combining cross-industry functionality, OASyS also offered load, distribution, power, and network management systems for electric utilities.

Metso Automation Is Formed

In 1999, the merger of Valmet and Rauma Corporation, another Finnish company, resulted in the formation of Metso Corporation, the world's leading supplier of fiber and paper technology processes and machinery. As a result of subsequent divisional restructuring,

MODERN CONTROL ROOMS, SUCH AS THE ONE AT WABASH VALLEY POWER ASSOCIATION, HAVE COME A LONG WAY SINCE THE EARLY DAYS OF SCADA, COMBINING FEATURES SUCH AS PROJECTOR SCREENS, ELECTRONIC MAP BOARDS, ERGONOMICALLY DESIGNED OPERATOR CONSOLES, AND WIRELESS COMMUNICATIONS.

METSO AUTOMATION PROVIDES REALTIME SOLUTIONS TO THE OIL, GAS, WATER/WASTEWATER, AND ELECTRIC UTILITY INDUSTRIES.

Valmet Automation and Neles Controls, a designer and manufacturer of valves and flow-measurement systems, were integrated into a new business group, Neles Automation, later renamed Metso Automation.

"The merger has made the resulting Metso Automation group a US$700 million concern," says Jardine. "This positions us nicely to compete internationally on a global scale."

As the new millennium unfolds, Metso Automation has implemented a new program for networking automation and information activities from the field to the enterprise: the Dynamic Network of Applications (DNA) strategy. This corporate-wide program integrates a number of RealTime decision-making components, including the @WEB solutions suite, which provides customers with a Web-enabled tool for accessing information anytime, anywhere.

"Our key thrust is to integrate the field and business environments," says Jardine. "In today's climate of deregulation and globalization, energy companies must provide value to their customers, and differentiate themselves based on characteristics such as quality, prompt delivery, and safety. To provide that value, they need RealTime access to field data. We provide the data, and trans-

form it into information that results in what we call 'actionable understanding'—the ability of the customer to take action."

Global Success

With a customer list including nearly half of the Fortune Global 500 petroleum companies, Metso Automation has delivered more than 500 integrated solutions to customers in North America and to every continent on the globe. Internationally, one of the company's most recent and challenging high-profile projects has been the Caspian Pipeline Consortium's US$2.2 billion, 1,500-kilometre pipeline, which runs from Kazakhstan to a new export terminal near the Black Sea. Metso Automation provided its SCADA system solution for the entire pipeline, as well as sophisticated simulation and modelling software for pipeline testing and operator training.

Superior products are not the only reason for the company's success. Metso Automation recently received national recognition for its employee initiatives when it was selected as one of Canada's top 100 employers. "Our greatest assets are our depth of knowledge and our people," says Jardine. "Our employees not only have strong technical skills, they also have expert knowledge of our

clients' businesses, which is a key requirement for ensuring successful customer partnerships. We're also fortunate to have strong export support from both the provincial and federal governments. We've been able to reach out globally, and now Metso is a world leader in SCADA and RealTime information management systems. It's a source of great pride for us."

Planning for the Future

Metso Automation's corporate mandate is to double the size of its business by 2005. Jardine says this growth will be accomplished through an integrated approach: continuing with core business initiatives; increasing the focus on developing markets being driven by deregulation, globalization, and new technology; and creating new solutions and strategies allowing Metso Automation to expand its technology reach inside the corporation. Based on the company's internal skills, technology resources, value architecture, and global partner network, which provide the corporate strength for collaborating with domestic and international clients over the long term, there is little doubt that Metso Automation will continue to be an industry leader for decades to come.

Profiles in Excellence

1979

1989

Lafarge Canada Inc.

hen travelling to Banff, one can't miss the cement plant 80 kilometres west of Calgary at the foot of Mount Exshaw. Lafarge Canada Inc. has been quarrying limestone from the mountain since 1970, but the Exshaw plant dates back to pre-World War I days, when Lord Beaverbrook's Canada Cement Co. Ltd. was created from the merger of 10 cement manufacturing companies. In 1970, the company became associated

with Lafarge Canada Inc., as we know it today.

Parent company to Lafarge Canada Inc., is U.S.-based Lafarge Corporation, whose majority shareholder is Lafarge SA in Paris. Founded in 1833, the company today employs more than 71,000 people in over 70 countries, and holds leading positions in each of its divisions: cement, aggregates and concrete, roofing, gypsum wallboard, and specialty products.

As the largest supplier of cement in Canada, Lafarge operates numerous plants throughout the country and is the only producer serving principal markets from coast to coast. The Exshaw plant produces more than 1 million metric tonnes of high-quality Portland Cement each year. Some cement is shipped as far away as Halifax and Alaska. Portland, masonry, mortar, and specialty cements are used in all aspects of residential, commercial, and public works construction.

Meeting the Demand

n addition to being a key employer in the Canmore-Bow Valley Corridor, Lafarge has numerous operations in and around the Calgary area, including Airdrie and High River. With an impressive network of skilled people and operations, the company offers customers access to a diverse selection of construction materials plus commercial, residential, and construction services. Lafarge has produced and supplied cement, ready-mix concrete, aggregates, asphalt, precast concrete, concrete pipe, and reinforcing steel to the construction industry for a long time. These products can be seen in many places—from sidewalks to schools and from houses

to high-rises. Lafarge's products were used in projects such as Banker's Hall, Ernst & Young Tower, Sheraton Suites Hotel, and Centre Street Bridge, to name a few.

Preserving the Environment

nvironmental protection is a key strategic objective for Lafarge—a commitment the company takes very seriously. With a firm belief that industrial development must create value, protect the environment, respect people and their cultures, and be sparing in its use of natural resources and energy, the company recycles materials, and cautionary measures are strictly adhered to. Future reclamation can be a bonus to neighbouring communities.

For instance, one former gravel pit along the Bow River will be transformed into a golf course, while other sites have been transformed into lakes fully stocked with fish.

Recycling is crucial at Lafarge. A prime example is the use of fly ash, a powder removed from flue gases during combustion of coal. In a long-standing, joint effort with Calgary-based TransAlta Utilities, Lafarge's Exshaw plant recycles TransAlta's fly ash and uses it as a raw material in the production of cement and as a supplemental cementing material used in the production of concrete. Fly ash can significantly enhance well-designed concrete, and provides benefits such as water reduction, improved workability and finishability, higher ultimate strengths, and greater overall economy.

A Small Large Company

As a leading provider of construction materials, Lafarge has financial strength, stability, and flexibility. Yet, despite its size, a decentralized structure allows the local team to work closely with customers and support the company's communities. It is this capability that supports the firm's goal of remaining its customers' supplier of choice. With this in mind, it is the shared know-how that makes Lafarge unique and creates its ability to provide customers with a competitive advantage. Motivated, skilled employees—the heart of the company—are key to its continued success.

Laudable Innovation

In a fast changing and competitive environment, Lafarge's ongoing challenge is to develop new innovations to better serve its customers. The company addresses needs by offering a strong combination of solutions, expertise, and reliability. Leading-edge technologies, a result of continued commitment to research, keep Lafarge and its customers at the forefront of the industry.

At the company's research and development laboratory in France, research is resolutely customer focussed and favours realistic, competitive innovations. The lab develops new products from raw materials and broadens the knowledge base. One notable, fairly recent development is Agilia®, a self-compacting performance concrete that offers an extremely smooth, bug-hole-free surface. Agilia is self-placing and self-levelling, and requires little or no vibration. Clients appreciate Agilia, a truly unique product, for the increased speed of construction it allows, as well as for its aesthetically pleasing finish.

To encourage innovation, Lafarge SA launched the Lafarge Innovation Awards in 1999. First prize was awarded to the company's Canadian Construction Materials group for development of a lightweight aggregate. Aptly named True Lite®, this product addresses the needs of concrete block manufacturers by offering advantages in weight reduction, fire resistance, sound attenuation, and thermal insulation. Additionally, the Western Cement Distribution team took third prize for its development of Trainspotter IT®, an award-winning rail car management tool. Faced with increasing logistics costs due to difficulty in predicting transit times for cement shipments, Lafarge Canada, in partnership with RADSS Technologies, developed Trainspotter, which allows each rail car to be traced and, therefore, its utilization optimized. Today, this leading-edge technology for bulk material rail shippers is fast becoming an industry standard.

Through its Cement and Construction Materials operations, Lafarge Canada proudly provides its customers with an unmatched wealth of products, services, and innovative ideas for the Calgary area and beyond.

Alberta Energy Company Ltd.

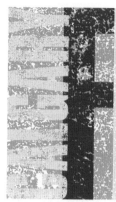

rom its inception as a Crown corporation in 1973, Alberta Energy Company Ltd. (AEC) has reinvented itself to meet the challenges of the ever volatile energy industry to become one of North America's largest independent oil and gas companies. AEC was initially created by the Alberta government to give Albertans the opportunity to participate directly in the development of the province's vast natural resources. It was clear from the beginning that AEC would act as a private sector company, and that the government's role would be limited to partial ownership—not management.

The company's first public offering in 1975 was oversubscribed, a huge success with more than 60,000 Albertans purchasing half the company through common shares at $10 each. It was one of the largest single share offerings in Canadian history, with the government still retaining 50 percent ownership.

In its early years, AEC acquired the oil and gas rights on the Suffield military base and the Primrose Air Weapons Range, both located in Alberta. "The company developed a unique expertise in the safe and environmentally sound exploration and development of oil and gas properties located within active military ranges," says Gwyn Morgan, President and CEO since 1994, and one of the company's earliest employees.

An International Player

The government gradually reduced its investment in AEC, and in 1993 all of its remaining shares were sold, again with a first preference to Albertans. Over the years, AEC made several smaller acquisitions of other companies or assets, but a milestone transition occurred in 1996, with the $1.1 billion merger with Conwest Exploration. This gave the company a major presence in Alberta's sour gas industry to complement its solid reserves and growing production of sweet gas. On the oil side, the acquisition of Amber Energy two years later added to the company's heavy oil assets in northern Alberta. AEC is also the second-largest owner of Syncrude, the largest oil sands plant in the world.

AEC's vision is to build a "global super-independent." In 1999, the takeover of Pacalta Resources provided AEC with the oil industry's strongest production position in the Oriente Basin of Ecuador. "Our first platform internationally is Ecuador, and we anticipate a great deal of low-cost growth," says Morgan. "But there also will be growing international investments in addition to Ecuador—in selected basins that are consistent with our mantra of growth, value, and performance." In addition to its Latin American operations, the company has a presence in the United States, Australia, and the Caspian Sea.

But moving into the international scene has not meant neglect for domestic holdings. AEC now ranks first in natural gas production in Canada and fifth among independent producers in North America. The company is also a major gas storage developer and pipeliner of conventional, synthetic, and heavy oil across North America.

AEC is organized into three divisions: international upstream oil and gas, domestic (North America) upstream oil and gas, and the midstream division that focuses on pipelines and gas storage. Each division features business units that are fully accountable for initiatives and performance. "This structure helps ensure that each division can respond quickly to potential opportunities," says Morgan.

The blend of upstream and midstream operations provides opportunities for numerous synergies. "One of the factors in our successful purchase of Pacalta was our pipeline experience," says Morgan. "We provided impetus to building an export pipeline in Ecuador."

The Top Employer

One of the most unique aspects of AEC is its corporate culture. With a clear vision of where it is heading, the company fosters and rewards employee entrepreneurship and initiative, and its employee incentive program fully supports a belief that there's no such thing as a bad idea.

According to a survey conducted by *Report on Business Magazine,* AEC was selected in 2000 as the third-best company to work for in Canada, and the firm tops among oil and gas companies. This ranking

ALBERTA ENERGY COMPANY LTD. (AEC) IS ORGA-NIZED INTO THREE DIVISIONS: INTERNATIONAL UPSTREAM OIL AND GAS, DOMESTIC UPSTREAM OIL AND GAS, AND THE MIDSTREAM DIVISION THAT FOCUSES ON PIPELINES AND GAS STORAGE.

was the result of an independent national evaluation sent to more than 500 companies, and included independent surveys of more than 250 employees.

The company takes a team approach to management, with the understanding that leaders are found at all levels of the organization. One of the first users of the 360-degree performance review, AEC employees receive feedback from their subordinates and peers, as well as their supervisors. Each employee in the company has his or her own goals and objectives, ultimately tied to shareholder value.

All employees have a stake in AEC. Long-term incentives tied to the AEC share price are used throughout the company. Performance is also recognized using shares. "And we're committed to providing the resources for all employees to reach their goals," adds Morgan.

The company has never participated in industry layoffs—highly unusual in the volatile oil and gas industry. Because the industry is cyclical, people skills can be applied elsewhere in the company, to continue to add value during downturn. The company's voluntary turnover rate of 4 percent is less than half the industry average.

A Company with Soul

AEC has been described as an employer with soul. Wherever it operates, the company takes its commitment to the environment seriously. AEC is determined to help reverse the negative environmental and social impacts of 25 years of exploration and development on Ecuadorian leases recently acquired by the company. "Our environmental practices are designed to set a new standard in the region—one that we hope that others will emulate," says Morgan.

In addition to its Employee Matching Gifts policy in North America, AEC supports more than 400 special community programs—with a focus on health, education, and youth—through initiatives like the Integrative Health Institute of Calgary, Alberta Tobacco Reduction Alliance, Manning Awards for Canadian Innovation, Canada-Wide Science Fair, and educational partnerships with selected high schools in the firm's operating regions. The company also fosters the concept of sustainable community development in the Oriente rain forest of Ecuador through Fundacion

NanPaz (www.nanpaz.com), which works with the indigenous people and migrant settlers who set up a home base in the region.

"Much of AEC's success can be summed up in the following philosophy: hire and reward the right people; instill in them the core values of the organization; give them clear goals, responsibility, and accountability; and then get out of the way," concludes Morgan. "That combination will be a major influence as AEC achieves its goal of becoming a global, super-independent." The company's Web site is www.aec.ca.

Cadillac Fairview Corporation Limited

What started in Toronto in 1953 as an idea—and an argument between friends—is today known as Cadillac Fairview Corporation Limited, one of North America's largest fully integrated commercial real estate operating companies. Three friends—Eph Diamond, Joseph Berman, and Jack Kamin—had just founded their own construction company, when one evening while meeting over dinner, a minor argument

developed over what to name their new venture. "When we went outside," recalled Berman, "Eph got into his car—a Cadillac. We all decided that would be a good name, though it got us into a fight with General Motors."

While the company still occasionally receives phone calls from eager car buyers mistakenly looking for a Cadillac, almost all Canadians will recognize at least some of the landmark structures operated by Cadillac Fairview Corporation. There are the Victoria and Toronto Eaton Centres, as well as Winnipeg's Polo Park, the Pacific Centre in Vancouver, and Fairview Pointe Claire in Montreal. Office buildings, too, are a large component of the company's portfolio. In March 2000, the outstanding

shares of the company were purchased by the Ontario Teachers' Pension Plan Board.

"Almost 85 percent of all Canadian consumers live within 10 miles of our shopping centres," says Ron Wratschko, senior vice president of Cadillac Fairview's western portfolio. A strong Calgary presence is part of the company's portfolio—a presence that has graced the city's landscape for more than 40 years. Calgarians are familiar with most of the company's well-known structures—Chinook Centre and Market Mall are two of the premier shopping centres in the city. The firm also owns the Shell Centre on Fourth Avenue, the CanOxy Building, and the Encor Building.

Named for the famous warm winds that waft over the Rockies, the Chinook Centre

has been a landmark in Calgary for more than 30 years. Built in the 1960s as one of the city's first enclosed shopping centres, the mall is making history again with the completion of a $300 million renovation.

A second level has been added to the Chinook Centre, increasing the number of retail outlets to 220. The new food court features a $750,000 art installation, a stage, and quiet seating areas in a parklike setting. "The food court is one of a kind in this country," says Wratschko. "It has a look and design that hasn't been seen in Calgary—or Canada—ever before."

Chinook is also the first Canadian shopping centre to work with theme areas. The creation of three zones—fashion, lifestyle, and family—with transitional courts in between,

CHINOOK CENTER, A WELL-KNOWN PROJECT OF CADILLAC FAIRVIEW CORPORATION LIMITED, HAS BEEN A LANDMARK IN CALGARY FOR MORE THAN 30 YEARS.

provides shopping convenience by grouping similar stores in each section. Each area has its own distinct décor and color scheme. An entertainment wing features a 16-screen Famous Players theatre complex and an IMAX theatre, as well as several restaurants and a full-size Chapters bookstore.

All Roads Lead to Market Mall

Shoppers in the northwest part of the city will also soon be enjoying a $50 million, 120,000-square-foot expansion taking place at Market Mall, subject to community and city council approval. Conveniently located just off three major arteries, including the Trans-Canada Highway, Market Mall attracts more than 7 million shoppers each year. In terms of sales, the mall is in a dominant position in the Calgary market.

Market Mall is a leader in the community as well. "It's the first choice for national promotions and media events," says Wratschko. "Each year the mall raises more than $260,000 for various charitable organizations."

Cadillac Fairview also takes its own community involvement commitment seriously. The company is currently sponsoring the Safe Haven Foundation, a new charity offering long-term care for homeless teenage girls. Cadillac Fairview is also a major sponsor for the Forzani Iron Man Golf Tournament, which raises funds for the Peter Lougheed Centre.

A Unique Awards Program

Cadillac Fairview Corporation has also initiated its own awards program, the ARC awards, to support the retail industry. Each year Cadillac Fairview honours entrepreneurs and their outstanding achievements in new retail concepts with a $50,000 award. These awards recognize the whole retail industry—not just Cadillac Fairview tenants.

Each shopping centre is encouraged to submit nominations to recognize its own entrepreneurs. A Calgary company was the third-year winner—Jugo Juice, located at Market Mall, was recognized for its originality and quality products.

"Calgary has consistently maintained strong retail sales—some 29 percent above the national average," says Wratschko. "The takeover by the Ontario Teachers' Pension Plan Board is an excellent compliment to our commitment to ongoing growth in real estate development."

As for the future of Cadillac Fairview Corporation, Wratschko says, "Our goal is to enhance the quality, size, and dominance of our franchise, while delivering exceptional financial performance and customer satisfaction programs. Our three-part growth strategy is to maximize the value of existing properties, undertake strategic acquisitions, and actively manage our capital structure."

CADILLAC FAIRVIEW—ONE OF NORTH AMERICA'S LARGEST FULLY INTEGRATED COMMERCIAL REAL ESTATE OPERATING COMPANIES—IS PLANNING A $50 MILLION, 120,000-SQUARE-FOOT EXPANSION FOR MARKET MALL (LEFT).

ENCOR PLACE, LOCATED IN THE HEART OF DOWNTOWN, IS ONE OF CALGARY'S PREMIER OFFICE PROPERTIES (RIGHT).

Oxford Properties Group Inc.

hen Calgary visitors experience the city's increasingly vibrant downtown life, one of the companies they can thank is Oxford Properties Group Inc. The Canadian property management company has played a major role in the revitalization of the downtown core of Calgary, as well as numerous other cities throughout Canada. 🍁 With high-quality assets totalling more than $3 billion, Oxford owns interests in more than 43 million square feet of office, retail, and industrial space in major Canadian cities. Some 68 million square feet of commercial properties are managed across the country.

With roots established in Edmonton in 1960, Oxford looked south to Calgary and saw much opportunity. The company began assembling lands during the late 1960s and early 1970s, and established its local office in 1974. Although Oxford's head office is now in Toronto, the Calgary office manages western Canadian operations, including the city where the company first began.

THE OXFORD PROPERTIES GROUP INC. GARNERED PRAISE IN ITS RESTORATION OF EATON CENTRE IN 1990 (LEFT).

THE ERNST & YOUNG TOWER, BUILT BY OXFORD IN 2000, ENJOYS STATE-OF-THE-ART TECHNOLOGY AND MAKES A STRIKING ADDITION TO THE CITY SKYLINE (RIGHT).

Current Holdings

e had a vision of assembling lands for a major downtown shopping centre," says John Smith, Senior Vice President, Western Canada, for Oxford Properties. "One of our original holdings was the Eau Claire lands down by the Bow River–42 acres that are an integral part of our roots."

But Eau Claire development came later. The company's first major undertaking was TD Square, which opened in 1977. Calgary's first urban shopping centre right in the heart of downtown on the Stephen Avenue Mall, TD Square includes three levels of retail space, comprising 226,000 square feet. TD Square also is home to two 32-storey office towers–the Home Oil and Dome towers–comprising 792,000 square feet.

Devonian Gardens is a major attraction at TD Square. This city operated indoor park lures lunchtime office workers, and often offers public entertainment in a quiet, pastoral setting.

TD Square was the first downtown complex that brought people to the core of the

city. The next Oxford development would wait until Calgary's economy was ripe. In 1988, the 46-storey, award-winning Canterra building opened with 821,000 square feet of prestigious office space. A strong presence in the city's skyline, the Canterra Tower was Oxford's first of many developments on the Eau Claire lands.

Environmentally Friendly

All of Oxford's buildings are considered state of the art from the time when they are built, however Canterra was built especially to be environmentally friendly. Canterra was certified ISO 14001 in 1996, and Oxford implemented an environmental management system for the building in 1998. Canterra won the Mayor's award for environmental excellence in 1997, as well as numerous awards over the years from the Building Owners and Managers Association.

In 1990, Oxford opened the award-winning Eaton Centre and the adjoining, 40-storey Canada Trust Tower with 618,000 square feet. An important part of the Stephen Avenue Mall, the Eaton Centre has four levels of retail space connected to the Eaton's store. The Eaton Centre is connected to the adjacent TD Square through a unique "fat bridge," with retail operations on the bridge providing a seamless transition between the two complexes.

"Holt Renfrew is situated in the historical part of the complex–the part that was actually the original Eaton's store," says Smith. "In keeping with Oxford's long-standing commitment to historical preservation, we dismantled the store brick by brick, and when the building was completed, we brought back the bricks to restore the façade."

Recent Construction and Acquisitions

Later acquisitions and construction by Oxford complemented the company's two main downtown clusters–TD Square and Eau Claire. "Having strategic core clusters of properties helps us ensure consistent management and better services for our tenants," says Smith.

In 1998, Oxford acquired the 33-storey Shell Centre, adjacent to the company's Eau Claire holdings. And in 2000, the company built the Ernst & Young Tower, just north of Canterra, on a portion of the Eau Claire lands. The building enjoys state-of-the-art technology, including telecommunications services and gas generators to supply its own electricity during peak periods. Two spires at the top of the Ernst & Young Tower light up at night, providing a striking addition to the city skyline.

Also in 2000, the company purchased Calgary Place, with two office buildings that include the Mobil Tower and the Metropolitan Conference facility. In addition to its 2 million square foot urban holdings, Oxford also manages a suburban group with similar square footage. The suburban group consists of 42 buildings of office, industrial, and quasi-retail space located primarily in the southeast and south central industrial areas.

But the company is especially proud of its role in revitalizing Calgary's downtown core. "We used Calgary as a model for revitalizing other cities," says Smith. "We would bring visitors here to show them what can be done."

As Calgary grows, Oxford expects to continue development of the Eau Claire lands, which have the potential for an additional 2 million square feet of development.

If the key to real estate success is "location, location, location," then Oxford will have a bright future in Calgary.

OXFORD'S FIRST MAJOR UNDERTAKING WAS TD SQUARE, WHICH INCLUDES THREE LEVELS OF RETAIL SPACE AND IS HOME TO TWO 32-STOREY OFFICE TOWERS (LEFT).

CANTERRA TOWER, ANOTHER OXFORD ENDEAVOR, WON THE MAYOR'S AWARD FOR ENVIRONMENTAL EXCELLENCE IN 1997, AS WELL AS NUMEROUS AWARDS OVER THE YEARS FROM THE BUILDING OWNERS AND MANAGERS ASSOCIATION (RIGHT).

VECO Canada Ltd.

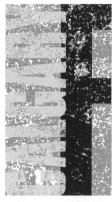

ounded in 1975 as a small, local consulting firm, VECO Canada Ltd. is today a private engineering company specializing in the design, engineering, and construction of oil and gas production, refining, and pipeline facilities, as well as power generation facilities. ❧ The company's first significant development came in 1981 when the firm, then known as Quantel Engineering Ltd., was contracted to handle engineering and construction for a major pipeline expansion by Peace Pipe Lines. In the next few years, Quantel began gaining recognition for its high-quality work in western Canada with major producers such as Shell, Esso, and British Petroleum (BP).

A Prosperous Decade

With the ability to lever off existing relationships, the company quickly grew to more than 100 employees. In 1990, the firm embarked on a strategic alliance with Gulf Canada Resources and obtained its first international project.

The KomiArcticOil Project in the Komi Republic of Russia inside the Arctic Circle provided the opportunity for the company to carry out feasibility studies; preliminary engineering; and detailed design of production facilities, pipeline gathering systems, field satellites, and related infrastructure. "The design and economic issues, combined with a severe climate and remote location, made this a very challenging project," says Doug Rogers, Senior Vice-President of the upstream oil and gas division.

Then followed another international opportunity—this time in the Middle East—for an acid gas recovery project in Abu Dhabi. By 1994, the company was focussing on developing its corporate vision and laying out a game plan to locate a strategic investor who could help the company secure larger, additional international contracts.

The desired financial boost came as a result of a merger with U.S.-based VECO Corporation in 1996. In 1998, the company acquired Calgary-based Quest, An Alliance Corporation, and Quest Industrial. Through this acquisition, VECO Canada began to provide engineering services for BP Amoco's natural gas group.

VECO Canada now employs more than 550 staff in Calgary and a further 200 in field offices in Vancouver, Bellingham, Houston, Italy, India, the United Arab Emirates, and Mexico. The company offers services in oil and gas gathering and processing, pipelines and terminals, petroleum refining, power generation, petrochemicals and sulphur recovery as well as an alliance division. In addition, VECO has also gained expertise in environmental clean-up technologies with an exclusive Canadian licence for the Superclaus sulphur recovery system.

"We have a well-balanced business portfolio, with 35 percent of our work being international," says Dave Stuart, VECO Canada President and General Manager. "This balanced approach ensures stability for our employees."

Recent projects include providing engineering services for environmental units for a $2 billion expansion at the Syncrude oil sands facility. This project is being undertaken in partnership with Fluor Daniel and SNC Lavalin. VECO also has a full engineering, procurement, and construction (EPC) contract for sulphur recovery units at Shell's new Upgrader at Scotford, northeast of Edmonton, in a joint venture with other EPC companies.

"We have lots of experience working in the Arctic—more than 30 years," says Stuart. "We've been involved in every major engineering and construction project in Alaska, including the world's largest gas plant, with a capacity of 8 billion cubic feet per day. As

DAVE STUART IS THE PRESIDENT AND GENERAL MANAGER OF VECO CANADA LTD.

the Arctic continues to be developed, we will be contributing our expertise on an ongoing basis to determine the most cost-effective ways to access north slope gas."

The company's newest area of expertise is power generation, a growth business with the current deregulation of the electric industry in Alberta, as well as other jurisdictions. In 1999 alone, VECO's power division obtained contracts for four major projects, including a waste heat recovery plant in Medicine Hat and a turnkey steam generator and turbine for TransCanada Power, one of the first independent power projects of its type in Alberta.

Partnering for Success

The company strives to live up to its motto—The Team that Delivers—by treating each client as unique. VECO spends time up front to determine the project's special parameters, whether they are tight deadlines or challenging engineering problems.

"The VECO team's performance in the Shell joint venture has been rated very highly by an independent, third-party auditor," says Stuart. "One of our hallmarks is our success in working with others. We do not go in and take over. Even if our partner is a competing firm, our policy is to work together and share the rewards, as well as the risks. Then our clients get the benefit of two sets of expertise—rather than just one."

There is a strong can-do attitude at VECO. The fact that the company is mentioned in the same breath with big multinational companies such as Fluor Daniel and Bantrel emphasizes its management talent and technology. A focus on trust and honesty, along with VECO's emphasis on continuing a family-style culture, has also clearly contributed to the company's success. The future is bright for VECO Canada Ltd.

Wingenback Inc.

or more than 25 years, Wingenback Inc. has been the general supplier to Canadian banks and industrial moving in Alberta, with a service-oriented attitude. The company got its start in 1975 when Al Wingenbach left an eight-year position with Diebold of Canada to move from Winnipeg to Calgary to start Wingenback Inc. His background with Diebold was in the sales, installation, and service of security equipment. The choice of Calgary was particularly important with its strong economy and regional head office for most of the major chartered banks. The company's mandate—Service Is Everything—has been and will always be the prevailing attitude.

Wingenback Inc. is truly a family-owned business, as it currently employs five brothers. The oldest brother, Al, currently CEO, started the business in Calgary, and Dennis joined him to head up the Edmonton office with its 1976 establishment, and currently heads up sales in Toronto. Youngest brother Wayne joined the company in 1978 and now serves as company president. Glen followed in 1990 and is the production director at the Crossfield facility. Perry came on board in 1996 and leads the project management division.

Moving Bank Equipment

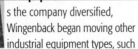s the company diversified, Wingenback began moving other industrial equipment types, such as printing presses. In addition, the firm manufactures and markets its own physical security equipment. By 1980 Wingenback had a solid foundation, with some 30 employees and a corporate office in northeast Calgary. The company was also taking advantage of its ties to the banking industry, noting the new focus on electronic banking after the construction of branch offices slowed in the 1970s and 1980s.

"There was no one in Canada building the surrounds and enclosures for ATMs, and the banks were having difficulties in dealing with U.S. suppliers," says Wayne Wingenbach. "We got into the business in 1990, and once we had our first order from a credit union, the big banks started to follow."

Wingenback opened a 50,000-square-foot manufacturing plant in Crossfield, Alberta, in 1995, to design and construct ATM surrounds using fibreglass, acrylic, wool, metal, and aluminum. Unique to Canada, the Crossfield plant is a source of pride for the company. A state-of-the-art airflow system eliminates paint odor and ensures a pleasant working environment for employees. The plant's location in a small town provides other benefits, including lower taxes, the ability to expand, and small-town living for workers.

Quality Products

he company's vast product line includes ATM surrounds and kiosks, self-service enclosures, security equipment, sign systems, and recreational items. Housings for all types of ATMs are available; exterior, interior, walk-up, and drive-up applications are accommodated, including retrofits, barrier-free surrounds, and designs for all models of ATM machines. Envelope units, waste units, shelves, and toe kicks are also integrated into the surround using various materials such as metal, marble-like solid surface, and rubber. The company works with clients to customize its products. Vinyl canopies, backlit signage, or custom backdrops are also available options.

Self-service enclosures specific to clients' requirements for information, interactive, and e-commerce purposes are designed and produced by Wingenback as exclusive or standard units. New or refurbished security items offer banking and credit union customers a variety of options for new or renovated branches. Wingenback's sign system division supplies a complete line of exterior and interior signs to meet specified requirements. Manufacturing capabilities and experience enable the company to produce these in addition to other items fulfilling its customers' needs.

A major turning point came in 1996, when the company received a contract from TD Bank for a three-year replacement program

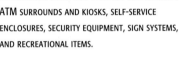

for all of its ATMs. "That contract took our company to a new level," says Wingenbach.

A Full-Service Approach

With more than 200 employees, Wingenback now provides a full-service approach in its niche market. There is a new office in Surrey, British Columbia, and the company manufactures its own fibreglass at a plant in Lethbridge. In addition to its moving division and surround manufacturing division, Wingenback also operates a project management and construction division to assist with the installation of ATMs and other banking equipment.

The company's project management team works hard on bidding for new projects across Canada and finding creative solutions for often difficult problems. The team works with the moving divisions, the manufacturing plant, and the sales and marketing team to bring projects from inception to completion.

Wingenback also provides an outdoor signage service for the local market. With its graphics, paint, and electrical capability, the Crossfield plant has the equipment and expertise to produce quality products, including backlit signs, awnings, and free-standing signs.

Yes-We-Can Attitude

If we say we can do it, somehow we've always managed to pull it off," Wingenbach says. "We figure out a way to get it done." With that kind of attitude, it's easy to see why the company maintains its market share in Canada. One of its strengths is having its own manufacturing facilities while other suppliers must outsource various functions.

"We have control over the whole process—from the initial concept to design, engineering, construction, transportation, and installation," says Wingenbach. "We're big enough to get the job done, but small enough to maintain hands-on control over everything." Wingenback Inc. is satisfied with its progress, but also focused on the future. Growing from a tiny, service-oriented operation to a sizable company, the firm has emphasized a philosophy of hard work and good service. Wingenback anticipates substantial expansion of its current business volume in the U.S. market in the near future.

WINGENBACK INC.'S VAST PRODUCT LINE INCLUDES ATM SURROUNDS AND KIOSKS, SELF-SERVICE ENCLOSURES, SECURITY EQUIPMENT, SIGN SYSTEMS, AND RECREATIONAL ITEMS.

THE COMPANY'S MANDATE—SERVICE IS EVERYTHING—HAS BEEN AND WILL ALWAYS BE THE PREVAILING ATTITUDE.

NovAtel Inc.

ovAtel Inc. has played an active role in making Calgary a world centre renowned for its expertise in global positioning systems (GPS). NovAtel is considered to be the industry's Canadian leader, as well as one of the top five companies in the industry throughout the world. ♣ NovAtel designs, markets, and supports a broad range of GPS products that provide location information from 24 earth-orbiting satellites transmitting

radio signals 24 hours a day worldwide. GPS receivers calculate the distance from a satellite to the receiver based on a triangulation technique to determine exact geographic locations. Applications include surveying, geographic information systems, agriculture, aviation, marine, and mining and machine control. These high-end markets represented about US$2 billion in 1999 and are expected to more than triple by 2003.

Founded by the Alberta Government in 1978, NovAtel went public in 1997. In 1998, BAE Systems Canada Inc., formerly Canadian Marconi Company, purchased 58 percent of the company's shares, becoming NovAtel's majority owner. BAE is a world leader in the design, manufacture, sales, and support of high-tech electronic products for the aerospace and communications industries.

In 1999, NovAtel and its strategic partner, Sokkia Co., Ltd., formed a jointly owned company called Point, Inc. This joining brought together NovAtel's world-class GPS engineering and Sokkia's unparalleled sales and distribution network with more than 25 subsidiaries throughout the world.

NovAtel also entered into a joint venture in 1999 to provide GPS products and services in Costa Rica and other Central American countries. The joint venture's first project involved a roadway study in Costa Rica, which will assist in the country's reinvestment in highway maintenance and construction.

From Aviation Navigation to Undersea Mapping

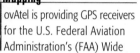 ovAtel is providing GPS receivers for the U.S. Federal Aviation Administration's (FAA) Wide

Area Augmentation System (WAAS). This aviation project involves converting navigation and instrument approach systems from radio-based to GPS, eventually eliminating the need for additional ground-based navigation aids. NovAtel has also received orders from other countries such as Canada, Japan, China, and Europe for similar initiatives.

"WAAS is the first step toward achieving an integrated worldwide global navigation satellite system, which will improve the safety and efficiency of international aviation," says Executive Vice President and Chief Financial Officer Werner Gartner.

Through Point, Inc., NovAtel is addressing the survey and geographical information system (GIS) markets with high-accuracy, easy-to-use products. Whether building a house in Calgary or a new road in Costa Rica, GPS offers advantages such as not needing a

IN EVERY OEM4 RECEIVER THERE IS AN APPLICATION WAITING TO GET OUT.

line of sight between land-based reference points. GPS is also lowering the cost while increasing the accuracy in GIS applications from ground contour maps to equipment data bases for utility companies.

NovAtel's GPS receivers also play an important role in increasing the accuracy and speed of mapping farms for site-specific farming, a new farming technique that involves subdividing large areas of farmland to determine precise fertilizer requirements, thereby improving crop yields and reducing costs.

Mining companies use GPS units to improve the accuracy of their drilling operations and shovel control. Security companies are also incorporating NovAtel's products into their work, using robotic vehicles that patrol exterior warehouses, fence perimeters, and open-pit hazardous waste storage sites.

The company's products also increase the accuracy of marine navigation. Seismic surveying, pipeline and undersea cable deployment, harbour channel dredging, and oil rig positioning all benefit from the extremely accurate measurements provided by NovAtel's receivers.

"Our technology offers the highest accuracy, integrity, and reliability," notes Gartner. "We're one of the few highly specialized GPS companies that can provide accuracy from one metre to the subcentimetre level."

Ongoing Research

In the high-tech GPS business, research is crucial and new products must be introduced every year. Because of this, the company is in a cycle of continuous innovation and new product development.

"New applications are being developed all the time," notes Gartner. "In addition to our strategic alliances with large companies, we enjoy working with inventors and entrepreneurs to make their dreams a reality."

NovAtel's research focuses on its core technology, creating products with better performance and more functionality at lower cost. The company has more than a dozen patents for new technology.

NovAtel employs approximately 110 people who must be highly educated and trained to help the company maintain its leading edge. The company works closely with the University of Calgary to ensure that proper training takes place.

The company has played a very active role with the Geomatics Engineering Program at the University, and senior management has been involved in the past with the Geomatics Advisory Council and with the major expansion of research facilities at the University to accommodate more research in multi-disciplinary engineering. The company also helped the University acquire a $400,000 GPS simulator.

NovAtel's involvement with the University is not totally altruistic, since graduates are hired on an ongoing basis. But the cooperation and leadership demonstrated reflect the company's strengths in all aspects of its business. These strengths will help NovAtel maintain its position as a world leader in the GPS industry.

"Calgary is an exciting place to be, and this is an exciting business to be in," says Gartner.

Media One Communications Limited

Incorporated in 1979, Media One Communications Limited specializes in advanced new media for business presentations. Working closely with Canada's leading corporations, the company designs programs and tools to help its clients communicate more effectively—internally and externally. ❧ Media One originally produced corporate videos and commercials. The firm was the first company in the city to embrace digital video editing, through the purchase of the highly acclaimed Avid

Media Composer, used to edit many major motion pictures. As technology became increasingly sophisticated over the years, the company broadened its scope, becoming the first to offer video-based, interactive multimedia design and production for business, in addition to traditional audio and video production.

Using the latest software, Media One's artists and programmers design full-color, motion, interactive technology for laptop presentations, desktop presentations, kiosks for trade shows, CD-ROMs, or DVDs.

Media One also develops highly evolved Web sites that use audio and video, as well as animated graphics, to both attract and keep visitors. Using the latest Web technologies, including Shockwave, Flash, and a wide range of video and audio technologies, the company is well positioned to offer enhanced content as the Web moves to a video-based medium in the future.

A Leader in Advanced Media

"Interactive technology is the most powerful communication tool yet developed," says Peter Temple, President. "It has helped clients increase sales closing rates by 70 percent, and it has helped build companies from the ground up, practically overnight. It is an incredible medium—it is flexible and fluid, and allows true interaction in a way that traditional media do not. We understand

its capabilities and have much more experience in working with the technology than other local companies."

A number of blue-chip companies obviously agree with Temple. Media One's current client list covers the Who's Who in Alberta, including the Alberta Government, Banff Centre, Calgary Herald, Canadian Association of Petroleum Producers, Deloitte & Touche, Petro-Canada, TELUS Advertising, PanCanadian, TransCanada

PipeLines (TCPL), Westjet Airlines, and VIP International.

Media One's high-tech approach can be used for a variety of different communication objectives, although interactive presentations are especially well suited for investor relations, marketing, and training. With these three applications, companies can see tangible results—whether those results are higher priced shares, increased sales, or acquiring new skills or information.

Investor Relations and Marketing

Media One provides a complete range of services in investor road show support—from initial script writing and presentation coaching to staging and video packaging. Media One produced the road show for Westjet when the company went public.

Media One also completed an interactive marketing presentation for a company offering off-site data backup services. The client was having a difficult time telling what was a complex story. Through the use of video in the computer presentation, potential customers could actually see the company's facility in operation and hear

INTERACTIVE MULTIMEDIA IS THE MOST POWERFUL MEANS OF COMMUNICATION YET DEVELOPED, ALLOWING THE USER TO ACCESS THE INFORMATION THEY NEED WHEN THEY NEED IT.

satisfied customer testimonials. Shortly after developing the presentation, the company was sold for $28 million.

Media One also prepared a marketing CD for the Banff Centre. "The Banff Centre is a conglomeration of about 10 buildings, and people often find it confusing," notes Temple. "Using Quicktime Virtual Reality, we are able to put the viewer right there. By providing 360-degree views, you can get a feeling for the depth of the rooms and their size. This is especially important for conference planners."

Proprietary Applications

Media One has also developed a number of proprietary applications that use this same interactive technology to make communication more efficient. Netlink provides hoteliers with the ability to instantly update their hotel room rates and availability on the global distribution system (GDS), so that travel agents can access them. The program was developed to provide a graphical user interface to an otherwise difficult-to-use, character-based program, and is now being used around the world.

Travel agents can provide clients with up-to-date pricing and visual information on hotels across North America with the new TravelView™ browser system. Connecting directly to major computer reservations systems, TravelView provides traditional text-based entry and instant access to maps of more than 200 major North American cities. Each map provides locations of major hotels, and clicking on a hotel provides pricing, availability information, and booking capability. Maps can be printed or e-mailed to a client, and include the hotel location, as well as the client's itinerary.

Training Applications

Media One has been designing video-based training for major Canadian corporations for some 25 years. Programs have ranged from technical to sales to management training. Since 1990, the company has pioneered interactive multimedia-based training in Calgary. Multimedia is especially well suited for training purposes. It allows individuals to proceed at their own pace and test their understanding of the material.

Turning gas jockeys into true "guest service attendants" was the mandate for a series of Petro-Canada training videos. Outcomes of this program included understanding the psychology of effectively dealing with customers and boosting sales as a result. The training videos were produced for staff across Canada in both English and French. Other Petro-Canada programs taught service station and environmental safety, as well as inventory and category management skills.

One of Temple's favourite projects was a CD titled "Lost

on the Farm," developed in partnership with Alberta Agriculture, TransAlta, and NOVA. Similar to a video game, "Lost on the Farm" features alien CyberSam, who crashes his spaceship on a farm and loses the special crystals needed to relaunch his spacecraft. Children play games that teach farm safety, ultimately finding the crystals that can send CyberSam home. The program won awards for design.

"There have been no models for how to produce these kinds of programs," says Temple. "We have needed to develop the methods and processes ourselves."

The most recent step for the company has been to move its multimedia technology onto the Internet. Clearly, Media One is leading the way—and changing how clients learn and how businesses communicate.

MEDIA ONE'S TEAM OF ARTISTS AND PROGRAMMERS WORKS ACROSS A WIDE RANGE OF MEDIA—FROM CORPORATE VIDEO TO INTERACTIVE MULTIMEDIA FOR THE WEB AND CD-ROM.

Fugro/SESL Geomatics Ltd.

What is now called Fugro / SESL Geomatics Ltd. started out as J. Stuart Engineering & Surveying Ltd. (Stuart Surveys) in August of 1980 with Jim Stuart as President and only employee. The residential housing market had just crashed and the oil industry was about to crash as Stuart Surveys started out. ❦ Being small was a blessing in an oil patch decimated by the NEP and low oil prices of the early 1980s.

The company was more competitive than bigger companies and did not need a big market share to be profitable. Thus SESL, whose original name was shortened to an acronym, grew in the 1980s with the like minded clients such as Renaissance Energy and Poco Petroleums.

When the oil patch ran into more troubled times in the late 1980s SESL was able to land the quality control of all survey services on the mammoth ALPAC Pulp Mill Project. Although this type of survey was different from the traditional oil patch requirements, SESL showed its versatility by working four years on this project with no cost overruns due to survey errors.

First in Russia

The 1990s saw the dissolution of the Soviet Union and the opening up of the newly independent countries to western technology. This, in turn, presented new opportunities to SESL. "We believe we were the first foreign surveying company in Russia in 1990," says Stuart. "We were working for Texaco on a big project in Northern Russia. We were also the first company to use global positioning system (GPS) technology in Russia, so it was a real groundbreaking experience. Of course, we had the KGB following us around all the time."

The company was able to obtain more work in Russia with Gulf Oil on the KomiArctic project and, later, in Khazakhistan with Canadian Occidental Petroleum. "There were lots of opportunities to work internationally, but we found we weren't quite big enough to compete for the larger contracts," says Stuart.

That led to discussions with Fugro Corporation, a multinational, Netherlands-based consulting firm seeking a geomatics presence in Canada. The Fugro group operates a worldwide network of land and offshore surveying companies, with more than 200 offices in some 45 countries. The takeover by Fugro was completed in July 1998, and the company has never looked back.

"We still operate totally autonomously, but now we have more stability, as well as the resources to go after more international work," says Stuart. "We are better able to weather the ups and downs of the oil and gas industry." Since acquiring SESL in 1998, Fugro has added Fugro Jacques Geo Surveys, based in St. John's Newfoundland and Fugro Airborne, based in Ottawa Ontario to its Canada group.

Current Operations

With approximately 90 employees, Fugro/SESL's mission is to be a total survey service provider for its clients. The company prepares oil and gas surveys; pipeline surveys; mapping and

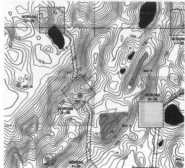

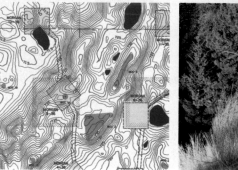

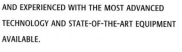

geographic information systems (GIS); construction and engineering surveys; mining surveys; and road, railway, and cadastral surveys. In order to be a broader service provider, the company has added project planning and project management, as well as database management, to its offerings.

Fugro/SESL's vision is to be the premier provider of surveying and survey engineering services to the oil and gas industry in the Western Canadian Sedimentary Basin. The company believes in extensive communication up front with clients to determine their needs. Then the best people—those who can deliver the best product—are assigned. Fugro/SESL takes advantage of technology where possible, encourages creative thinking, and works to provide value-added services.

With the advent of numerous technological innovations, Fugro/SESL has been quick to embrace the high-tech approach. "The survey industry has evolved in the past decade from one that was originally labor based to one that is now technology based," says Stuart. "We were one of the first companies to use GPS commercially. With the latest technology, it might take one month to complete a project that used to take up to six months."

All Fugro/SESL professionals are trained and experienced with the most advanced technology and state-of-the-art equipment available. Crews are equipped with total stations—data collectors, GPS receivers, and computers—to collect, process, verify, and relay data on-site. In addition, sophisticated CAD and GIS systems provide clients with integrated, detailed, and meaningful visual presentations.

One of the top survey companies in Alberta, Fugro/SESL has offices in Lloydminster, Alberta; Regina and Swift Current, Saskatchewan; Yellowknife, Northwest Territories; and a joint venture office in Khazakhistan, in addition to its Calgary headquarters.

"We're just a small survey company that's worked worldwide, but we've done some jobs no else thought were possible," says Stuart. "We have proved that Canadian survey technology can be applied anywhere in the world."

THE COMPANY'S MISSION IS TO BE A TOTAL SURVEY SERVICE PROVIDER FOR ITS CLIENTS.

A Focus on the Future

The company's worldwide experience has given it a unique knowledge of the oil patch and the application of survey skills. In addition to increasing its percentage of international work, Fugro/SESL will continue its focus on the North. In the past five years, the company has surveyed a good portion of the wells in the Northwest Territories. "The North is the last Canadian frontier," says Stuart. The company also hopes to obtain more work in the United States, with Fugro's ability to open some doors.

"At Fugro/SESL, we value and respect our clients' knowledge," says Stuart. "Their experience and understanding complement our technological expertise, and this results in a mutually beneficial relationship. We're prepared, equipped, and committed to providing geomatic service of the highest quality. And we welcome the opportunity to work with our clients and show them how trust, technology, and teamwork can lead to success."

Clearly, the next 20 years should be as successful as the first 20 for Fugro/SESL.

FUGRO/SESL GEOMATICS PREPARES OIL AND GAS SURVEYS; PIPELINE SURVEYS; MAPPING AND GEOGRAPHIC INFORMATION SYSTEMS (GIS); CONSTRUCTION AND ENGINEERING SURVEYS; MINING SURVEYS; AND ROAD, RAILWAY, AND CADASTRAL SURVEYS.

DeVry Institute of Technology

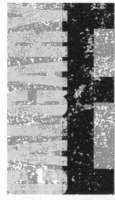

Established in Calgary in 1981, DeVry Institute of Technology is part of a private, post-secondary educational system of over 40,000 students that operates a growing number of campuses throughout North America. The Calgary campus, just off Barlow Trail at Memorial Drive and only minutes from downtown, offers bachelor degree programs in Business Operations, Computer Information Systems, and Electronics Engineering Technology, in addition to a diploma program in Electronics and Computer Technology.

Current trends, such as the ever expanding global marketplace and the increasing role of information technology, have placed intense pressure on post-secondary institutions to produce graduates with relevant knowledge, skills, and broader abilities. DeVry recognizes the importance of meeting the quickly changing demands of the workplace, and consequently makes demands of itself to be a leader in post-secondary curriculum development.

"We have always followed a business model approach," says John Ballheim, president of DeVry-Calgary. "Once the employers' needs have been identified, curriculum changes can occur as quickly as the following term."

Responsive to Employers' Needs

Changes, such as curriculum modifications, are not made in isolation. DeVry works closely with the business community, and considers employers one of its primary customers. A cross section of employers comprises DeVry's advisory boards for each program. These advisory boards help give a real-world perspective to the educational experience. When modifications or a new program are needed, special task forces of business representatives work with DeVry to develop the curriculum.

"Our fingers are on the pulse beat of the Calgary and Western Canadian business community," says Ballheim. "Because our success depends on their success, we stay in close touch with business needs."

In addition to structured activities for program development, one-on-one communication between DeVry staff and employers is ongoing and essential. "In our data base, we have thousands of employers, located not only in Calgary, but in Canada and the rest of North America," says Ballheim. "In any given week, our staff is in contact with hundreds of business contacts."

Students Are Customers, Too

Of course, a strong student focus is part of DeVry culture as well. Students who are attracted to DeVry are seeking to develop both their knowledge and employment skills. And they expect to see results. "We value our students

THE CALGARY CAMPUS OF DEVRY INSTITUTE OF TECHNOLOGY OFFERS BACHELOR DEGREE PROGRAMS IN BUSINESS OPERATIONS, COMPUTER INFORMATION SYSTEMS, AND ELECTRONICS ENGINEERING TECHNOLOGY, IN ADDITION TO A DIPLOMA PROGRAM IN ELECTRONICS AND COMPUTER TECHNOLOGY.

and motivation. Often parents, guardians, and spouses are included in these interviews.

In an effort to create a more well-rounded, employable graduate, all of DeVry's programs include a strong complement of general education courses. With the assistance of career advisers, most DeVry graduates find employment very quickly. During the last decade, thousands of students graduated from DeVry-Calgary. For the 10-year period ending February 1999, more than 90 percent of these graduates earned positions in their field of study within six months of graduation.

A Vital Member of the Community

DeVry makes an important contribution to Calgary by providing employers with qualified graduates who possess both strong interpersonal skills and the ability to apply their knowledge and skills to the workplace. Staff members are also encouraged to participate in the community through volunteering. As the immediate—and very active—past president of the Calgary Chamber of Commerce, Ballheim practices what he preaches.

"We support volunteerism and recognize our employees who make significant personal contributions through their community activities," Ballheim says.

"DeVry's commitment is for the long term. We made the decision to come to Calgary during the boom times of the late 1970s," says Ballheim. "We saw that Calgary was, as it still is, a center of growing influence in Canada—a dynamic, future-oriented city. The city's entrepreneurial approach, combined with its wonderful natural setting, clean air, and safe environment hold great promise for the future. We want to be part of that future. We have a role to play in making Calgary a viable player in the global economy for our faculty, staff, students, and alumni."

and hold ourselves accountable to them," Ballheim says.

To complement the educational program, students are offered a variety of services, such as help in finding a part-time job, housing assistance, and financial aid assistance. Course schedules are set up so students can attend classes in either the morning or the afternoon, allowing time for a part-time job. DeVry students also have the benefit of year-round education, allowing them to complete a four-year bachelor's degree program in three years or less.

DeVry conducts a personal interview with each prospective student to determine his or her academic background, interests,

TO COMPLEMENT THE EDUCATIONAL PROGRAM AT DEVRY, STUDENTS ARE OFFERED A VARIETY OF SERVICES, SUCH AS HELP IN FINDING A PART-TIME JOB, HOUSING ASSISTANCE, AND FINANCIAL AID ASSISTANCE.

DEVRY MAKES AN IMPORTANT CONTRIBUTION TO CALGARY BY PROVIDING KNOWLEDGEABLE WORKERS THAT EMPLOYERS NEED.

Pillar Resource Services Inc.

he story goes that one of the founders of Pillar Resource Services Inc. loved Caterpillar bulldozers so much that he named the company after the world-famous field equipment manufacturer. The association is not as unconnected as it might seem, since like its namesake, Pillar has built its reputation and success on its field expertise. ❦ "Most of our staff have a strong mechanical and/or technical ability, and they are inspired by self-motivation," says Joe Samaska, President. "They relate to people very well and they understand what it takes to keep a customer satisfied. By having a good balance of skills in the company, we are able to focus on the level of service desired by each of our customers."

Pillar employees, with their commitment to fairness and entrepreneurial drive to succeed, have helped the company weather the ups and downs of the volatile oil and gas industry since the firm first began operations in 1983.

Pillar offers the oil and gas industry a full range of services associated with the installation, modification, and fabrication of conventional oil and gas processing facilities such as gas plants, oil batteries, compressor stations, and well sites. Pillar also works closely with the heavy oil side of the petroleum industry with the installation, modification, and relocation of heavy oil treatment facilities, water treatment facilities, steam injection plants, and generators.

The Fight against Time

All of our staff in the field, the fabrication facility, and our offices have the ability to be flexible—to do what needs to be done, when it needs to be done," Samaska says. "That's very important in this line of work, since we're often working with tight deadlines that are imposed by our customers, as well as by the environment we are working in. A good example of this type of deadline occurs every spring when the frost leaves the ground in western Canada, and many rural roads and highways face restricted usage. With this in mind, our staff often work longer hours, in conjunction with our customers, in order to get as much done as possible before these restrictions are put into place."

Another deadline that is taken seriously by Pillar and its customers is the caribou run that occurs every spring in northern Alberta.

IN MANY WAYS, PILLAR RESOURCE SERVICES INC. AND ITS EMPLOYEES REFLECT THE VALUES AND CHARACTERISTICS OF THE COMPANY'S HEAD OFFICE HOME, THE CITY OF CALGARY—BOTH ARE FLEXIBLE, INNOVATIVE, ENTREPRENEURIAL, AND OPEN TO NEW IDEAS.

Here again the company's staff work closely with customers, adjusting Pillar's schedules to ensure the work is completed before the caribou start their journey. Minimizing any impacts to the environment has always been a real concern for the company.

With this kind of commitment, Pillar has developed a reputation as a leader in its field. The complexity and size of projects the company handles has increased dramatically, yet Pillar maintains a professional focus on each project regardless of its size.

One way to gauge a service company's success is to consider the number of its repeat customers. At least 70 percent of Pillar's customers are repeat business. With a new customer, Pillar will usually be awarded a contract on a competitive bid basis. With existing customers, this process is modified somewhat to enable the company to be involved in a dialogue very early on in the process, to ensure implementation is as efficient as possible. "We believe we can provide value-added expertise to help our customers achieve their goals," notes Samaska.

Continuing to Increase Value

Samaska and his colleagues understand that to continue to grow and prosper, companies must continue to offer more value. "These days our customers, the oil and gas companies, are required to perform for shareholders on a month-to-month basis, not year to year," Samaska says. "To support our customers, we look for leverage to deliver lower-cost, more streamlined implementation processes."

One way to achieve that leverage has been the company's investment in the latest technology for all areas of Pillar's operations; encouraging education and top performance from staff is another. Pillar's management works hard to understand the different groups of employees–office, technical staff, and trades–and what motivates them. Recognition of employees' performance is tied directly to their daily responsibilities and how well they handle these duties.

"Our staff is one of our major competitive advantages," says Samaska. In addition to flexibility, Pillar's employees need to be very well organized. Good communication skills, especially listening skills, are important, as is the need for diplomacy. "Occasionally when time deadlines are tight, emotions can run high, so our staff receive a lot of coaching on identifying issues and how to resolve them with customers," Samaska says.

In many ways, Pillar and its employees reflect the values and characteristics of the company's head office home, the city of Calgary. Like Calgarians, Pillar's employees are flexible, innovative, entrepreneurial, and open to new ideas. With a positive attitude and lots of energy, both Calgary and Pillar can look forward to a bright future in the coming years.

PILLAR EMPLOYEES, WITH THEIR COMMITMENT TO FAIRNESS AND ENTREPRENEURIAL DRIVE TO SUCCEED, HAVE HELPED THE COMPANY WEATHER THE UPS AND DOWNS OF THE VOLATILE OIL AND GAS INDUSTRY SINCE THE FIRM FIRST BEGAN OPERATIONS IN 1983.

At first glance, xwave is a classic information technology (IT) company with cutting-edge technology solutions. More than that, xwave is a truly unconventional company with a vibrant, people-centred corporate culture. Launched in January 1999 from four dynamic and profitable companies, xwave has grown to more than 2,300 people and revenues of more than $300 million. The company grew through an aggressive and ongoing strategy of mergers and acquisitions. One of the original four companies that formed xwave was Minerva Technologies, which was founded in Calgary in 1985.

The key to xwave's success has been its four guiding principles: focus, passion, people, and results. xwave is consistently building a vibrant corporate culture that engages people who deliver results.

"While other IT providers struggle to be all things to all people, we've spent our professional lives focusing on clients in industries where we have extensive experience," says Gord Forbes, Vice President, Western Business Unit. "Our expertise lies in combining our technical ability with an in-depth knowledge of the client's business. Our understanding allows us to develop innovative solutions to address the client's unique needs."

Areas of Expertise

Xwave offers extensive experience in telecommunications, energy, and select areas of the public sector, including defence, public safety, aerospace, and air traffic management. With 170 employees, the Calgary office provides its clients with end-to-end solutions—from system integration and software engineering right through to infrastructure services and product fulfilment.

About one third of the workload involves outsourcing, including infrastructure maintenance, network and desktop support, and application management. "We have a different model than our competitors when it comes to outsourcing," says Forbes. "Most IT providers take over the entire IT function for a client. However, we encourage the client to retain core functions, so they never lose control."

According to Forbes, this approach gives clients the best of both worlds—access to the best skills and the ability to ramp up or down quickly, depending on the environment. xwave understands the dynamic and cyclical nature of the oil and gas industry, and can handle IT impacts during periods of growth, stability, or restraint.

Customized Solutions

In addition to outsourcing, xwave also provides customized IT solutions for its clients, as well as e-business expertise. A unique aspect of the company is its focus on co-integration. Most IT service providers focus on either operational/field systems or corporate information systems. xwave works across both operational and corporate areas to bring solutions that address clients' total needs and help them realize larger opportunities.

"There was a time when many people believed that having corporate and operational systems working together was an unattainable dream," says Forbes. "To us at xwave, it's now a reality. Co-integration provides real business value. First, clients achieve better results in a shorter time frame. Second, they only need to deal with one company to address all their IT needs. Third, our approach helps clients identify opportunities for new services."

One of those new services is e-business, an area in which xwave has significant expertise. The company's co-integration approach facilitates e-business solutions, since electronic commerce often requires both operational and corporate information systems. xwave has carried out e-business work in most of Calgary's industry sectors.

"Most businesses today have an e component," says Forbes. "It may be only a static Web page or a fully interactive site where customers can purchase products or services.

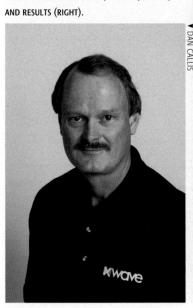

GORD FORBES, VICE PRESIDENT, WESTERN BUSINESS UNIT AT XWAVE SAYS, "OUR EXPERTISE LIES IN COMBINING OUR TECHNICAL ABILITY WITH AN IN-DEPTH KNOWLEDGE OF THE CLIENT'S BUSINESS" (LEFT).

THE KEY TO XWAVE'S SUCCESS HAS BEEN ITS FOUR GUIDING PRINCIPLES: FOCUS, PASSION, PEOPLE, AND RESULTS (RIGHT).

▼ DAN CALLIS

For many companies, e-business provides an additional distribution method for their products."

Special Applications

Xwave has helped oil and gas clients and power utilities attain goals of efficiency, growth, and profit. The company has developed and supported sector-specific applications in the areas of petroleum exploration, production, transportation, refining, retail, and more. xwave's work with power utilities has helped clients upgrade their systems, introduce new and more efficient technologies, and plan the integration and evolution of their systems. Notable clients include Talisman Energy, Unocal Canada, PanCanadian, TransCanada PipeLines, Husky Oil, Ontario Power Generation, TransAlta, and New Brunswick Power.

The company's portfolio of custom-developed oil and gas software includes systems for North American gas marketing, corporate jet flight reservation, environmental compliance assessment, royalty trust distribution, seismic tracking and recording, and customer information.

"We also have a lot of expertise in secure communication," says Forbes. "That area can have a number of applications, including offshore oil rigs wanting to transmit proprietary information to their head office, as well as secure financial transactions for e-business."

xwave is working to build its image in Calgary. The company is a major Stampede sponsor, supplying services in kind. In addition, xwave sponsors the annual Calgary Stampede Run-Off, and participates in the local Corporate Challenge. In 1999, the company established an even stronger presence in Calgary through the acquisition of Minerva Technology.

"We have a strong local presence and a reputation as a very capable, full-service IT consulting firm," says Forbes. "And xwave's slogan—We're on Your Wavelength—shows that we're focused on helping our clients succeed."

XWAVE IS A PROUD SPONSOR OF THE CONNELLY RACING TEAM.

XWAVE SPONSORED AN EXHIBIT AT COMDEX 2000.

SMART Technologies Inc.

SMART Technologies Inc., one of Calgary's entrepreneurial success stories, was founded in 1987 as the Canadian distributor for a U.S. projector company. Income generated through projector sales was allocated to fund R and D for an innovative new product: a touch-sensitive, interactive whiteboard called the SMART Board™. From those humble beginnings, SMART now manufactures its Roomware™ products, which include hardware and

software solutions to help groups access and share the information they need to meet, teach, train, and present.

SMART is led by the husband-and-wife team of David Martin, Chairman, and Nancy Knowlton, President. Right from the start, the duo had a vision of selling their unique products to markets around the world. "We sold our products for over two years in the United States before we completed a sale in Canada," says Martin. "With only limited resources early on to promote our products, we needed the larger market in the U.S. to get the greatest return."

In fact, 95 percent of SMART's products are exported. Approximately two-thirds of the company's products are sold in the United States, with the rest in Europe, Asia, Latin America, the Middle East, and, of course, Canada. SMART's unwavering commitment to quality and its ISO 9001 registration serve its global customer base with high-quality, reliable products.

The company's first product, the SMART

Board, is an interactive whiteboard that works with a computer and projector to allow presenters to write notes on the Board and save them to a computer file for future reference or distribution. Meeting or class participants can press on the touch-sensitive surface of the Board to control projected Windows or Macintosh applications, run multimedia materials such as CD-ROMs, or navigate the Internet directly from the Board.

SMART Boards are available in a variety of different formats: the SMART Board, the *Rear Projection* SMART Board, and an interactive overlay for plasma display panels, all powered by SMART Board Software. Since upgraded software is offered free from SMART's Web site, customers can maximize the effectiveness of their existing Roomware tools without added expense.

In addition to the SMART Board line of products, the company produces mobile multimedia cabinets that enable users to work seamlessly with peripherals, computer-lab instruction software that creates a focused

learning environment, and an optical whiteboard capture system that records notes written on conventional whiteboards.

SMART Applications

SMART products have a number of applications. For teachers and instructors, the SMART Board is an ideal classroom tool. Teachers often use SMART Boards as a window to the Internet. Rather than having a group of students clustered around a small computer screen, teachers can project images onto the Board so that students can easily see and navigate through sites with the touch of a finger. Companies use SMART Boards for computer application and soft-skills training. Organizations also use the SMART Board in meetings, enabling people to collaborate easily and efficiently.

SMART continually strives to improve upon its award-winning products. Each year new features are added in response to advances in technology and changing customer needs. That responsiveness has been key to the

company's success, according to Knowlton. "Customers were asking for the Board to recognize handwriting," says Knowlton. "Initially we recommended applications that they could buy and use with our product. But, pretty soon, we were integrating that function right into our software."

Customer Satisfaction

SMART's responsiveness to customer needs has played a key role in the company's high double-digit annual growth rate. "Customers who bought one or two units last year are now placing larger orders," says Knowlton. SMART Technologies has also focused on cost-reduction strategies to enable the company to offer the best pricing.

SMART Technologies continues to receive recognition from the business community in Alberta and across Canada. For a number of years, the company has been named one of Canada's 50 Best Managed Private Companies and one of Alberta's fastest-growing companies. In 2000 SMART was selected as Canada's Exporter of the Year by the Department of Foreign Affairs and International Trade.

As part of the company's commitment to giving back to the community, SMART Boards have been donated to all post-secondary institutions in Alberta and many others across Canada. In 1997 SMART founded the SMARTer

Kids™ Foundation, a private, not-for-profit organization dedicated to providing grant programs and other initiatives that enable schools to place technology into classrooms. A special focus of the Foundation is to provide opportunities—by placing technology and programs at their service—for teachers and children to learn new skills and grow in self-confidence. Tens of thousands of classrooms

have benefited from SMARTer Kids Foundation programs.

SMART is committed to providing quality, cutting-edge products to help people meet, teach, train, and present. And when people talk of Calgary's entrepreneurial spirit and can-do attitude, it's as clear as the writing on the whiteboard that SMART Technologies leads the way.

COMPANIES USE SMART BOARDS FOR COMPUTER APPLICATION AND SOFT-SKILLS TRAINING. ORGANIZATIONS ALSO USE THE SMART BOARD IN MEETINGS, ENABLING PEOPLE TO COLLABORATE EASILY AND EFFICIENTLY.

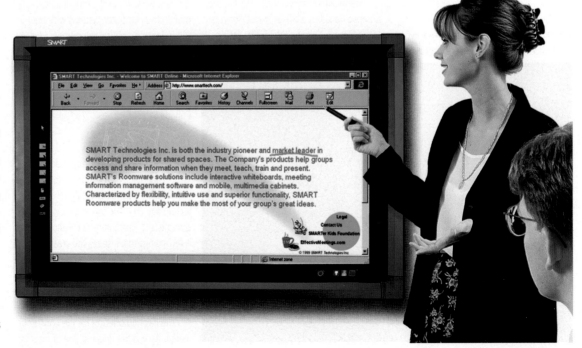

Compaq Canada Inc.

ased in Houston, Compaq Computer Corporation was founded in 1982. During its first decade, Compaq helped spark the emergence of the personal computer marketplace, becoming one of the world's largest suppliers of PC and server products in the 1990s, with some of the industry's most innovative, value-oriented desktop, portable, workstation, server, and peripheral PC technologies. ❧ Compaq has moved aggressively and decisively in the

21st century as a worldwide PC industry leader and the second-largest computer company in the world. The company has addressed the evolving challenges of today's commercial and consumer customers while maintaining the quality hallmark it established in the 1980s.

Compaq has established a reputation as a market share leader in industry-standard computing through its Windows NT®, SCO Unix, and NetWare® solutions. The company has added to its leadership in high-performance, 64-bit technology with Alpha® and Tru64 Unix®. Also, Compaq has committed to maintaining its lead in continuously available business-critical solutions by continuing its investment in OpenVMS™ and NonStop™ Himalaya, and by using the technologies of these platforms to fuel the development of industry-standard enterprise solutions.

Compaq Canada

ompaq Computer Corporation today sells and supports its products in more than 100 countries, with the assistance of more than 65,000 employees and 40,000 marketing partners. Compaq Canada Inc. is the fourth largest of the 34 international subsidiaries.

Headquartered in Richmond Hill, Ontario, Compaq Canada is a wholly owned subsidiary with offices in Calgary, Edmonton, Halifax, London, Markham, Mississauga, Moncton, Montreal, Ottawa, Quebec City, Regina, St. John's, Vancouver, Victoria, and Winnipeg.

Although the company's presence in the city predates its establishment in 1988, the Calgary office is home to more than 400 employees through Digital Equipment and Tandem Computers, which were both subsequently acquired by Compaq. These companies helped expand Compaq's capability beyond their initial PC market. Digital provided expertise in enterprise computing and professional services, while Tandem brought fault-tolerant mainframe computer systems with built-in redundancy for critical operations.

"Calgary is the hub for our western Canadian operations—from Thunder Bay to Victoria and from Lethbridge to Yellowknife," says Andy Canham, Vice President of Western Canada Sales.

Three Business Groups

hese days Compaq describes itself as a company that goes beyond providing information technology (IT). The more important story is another IT—inspiration technology, which is technology that inspires the creativity of its customers. To that end, the company has structured itself into three global business groups: Consumer, Commercial Personal Computing, and Enterprise Solutions and Services.

The flagship offering for the consumer marketplace is the Presario line of Internet PC's, designed for ease of use, management, and support. For commercial PC products, Compaq offers a range of equipment, including desktops, laptops, personal decision assistants, and iPaq wireless devices.

Network computing is the primary hardware offering of the Enterprise Solutions and Services Group, with three server platforms—each with a different level of reliability, depending on the organization's needs. The most popular platform is the Proliant, which runs Windows 2000 and has captured a 42 percent market share in Canada. The Himalaya server is intended for organizations that require absolute reliability, such as the stock exchange.

Alpha is the company's high-performance server for large-scale commercial enterprises. The U.S. Department of Energy's National Nuclear Security Administration selected Compaq to build the world's fastest and most powerful supercomputer based on the Alpha platform. With 12,000 Alpha processors, the computer is approximately the size of five basketball courts.

Compaq is also a world leader in enterprise storage. Storage is expected to fuel Compaq's enterprise computing growth well into the future.

The Enterprise group also offers technical and professional services to large organizations, including the design, building, and implementation of computer systems

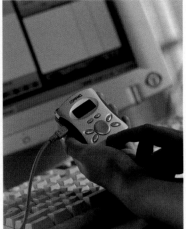

and solutions, as well as management and technical services.

Centre of Excellence

The company has established a worldwide centre of excellence for technical consulting and support in Calgary. On call 24 hours a day, seven days a week, the centre offers the expertise of some 150 employees to many local and international companies such as Bell South and New York's Citibank.

"We chose Calgary as the location for the centre since it provides access to the skills we need," says Canham. "We're truly creating jobs here, not just taking over other companies' employees when they decide to outsource."

Compaq has a strategic partnership with the City of Calgary, and works with Petro-Canada, TransAlta, TCPL, and PanCanadian, to name only a few. "There are very few large companies that we don't do business with," Canham says. In addition, Compaq has hundreds of partners in Calgary who resell or repackage the company's products and services for the consumer and commercial marketplace.

Compaq is ensuring that its presence in Calgary is felt in a number of ways. In addition to its new office tower on Fifth Avenue downtown, the company actively supports a number of community initiatives. For example, Compaq donated approximately $40,000 worth of equipment for the start-up of the Calgary

Prostate Cancer Foundation. A major sponsor of the Calgary Flames, Compaq helped launch the Flames Forever initiative to keep the hockey team in the city. And through a partnership with the University of Calgary, the company has provided equipment for the school's Multimedia Advanced Communication Initiative.

As society continues to develop the world of e-commerce, Compaq has vowed to help facilitate that transition. "Customers need an IT partner who can deliver simple and useful computing solutions that truly empower them in the 'Internetworked' world," says Compaq Canada President David Booth. "We have everything we need to be that partner—one of the best computing companies in the world."

QSound Labs, Inc.

Widely recognized as the pioneer of digital 3D audio technology, QSound Labs, Inc. was founded in Calgary in 1988. The company's founders began experimenting with multiple microphone arrays in the early 1980s, discovering that sound could be made to appear to come from different directions, well beyond the normally restrictive stereo image–much like the way in which the human ear detects sound locations naturally.

After securing research capital, QSound assembled a team of scientists who invested thousands of hours during the 1980s in the development of powerful custom software tools that utilized the newly available power of digital signal processors, as well as desktop computers. After administering more than 500,000 listening tests, to better understand the way a human ear perceives directional sound, the company delivered a technological coup–the world's most natural-sounding, effective 3D audio algorithms for stereo speakers. The technology is protected by 16 U.S. patents.

Audio Applications

Using its proprietary technology, QSound has developed 3D audio applications for virtual surround sound, positional audio, and stereo enhancement. The company's cutting-edge, 3D audio technology allows consumers to enjoy high-quality, realistic, three-dimensional stereo surround sound with just two speakers.

The company's business partners include such top industry names as AIWA, Kodak Mitsubishi, Oak, Philips, RealNetworks, Sanyo, Sharp, and Starkey Laboratories. QSound's partnerships have resulted in widespread use of its technology in motherboards, sound cards, consumer electronics products, Internet audio software, and hearing aids.

"Although most of our customers are large multinationals based in the U.S. and Asia, QSound-enhanced TVs, PCs, and hearing aids are available in Canada," says Gallagher, President and CEO.

In keeping with its global audience, and since most of its shareholders are based in the United States, the public company is listed on the NASDAQ stock exchange.

Four Main Applications

QSound's 3D audio technology is being applied in four main areas: the PC/multimedia industry, consumer electronics, Internet audio, and health care. In the health care arena,

the company has focussed its efforts on licensing its technology to the largest worldwide hearing aid manufacturer, Starkey Laboratories.

QSound applied its expertise and experience in sound and software to create a binaural hearing aid based on digital algorithms that restore a user's ability to listen selectively in noisy places. Traditional hearing aids simply crank up the volume, which actually impedes the brain's efforts to determine direction.

QSound's stereo enhancement and surround sound 3D audio technologies are incorporated by major manufacturers into their products, including DVDs, minicomponent systems, speakers, stereos, televisions, and VCRs. Some of the major industry leaders who build and sell these products globally are AIWA, Boston Acoustics, Sharp, and Toshiba.

QSound's consumer Internet audio software products have become the standard in sound enhancement for streaming audio on the Internet, adding rich, 3D

THROUGHOUT THE YEARS, QSOUND'S TECHNOLOGY HAS BEEN USED BY PROMINENT RECORDING ARTISTS, IN MAJOR MOVIE SOUNDTRACKS, AND ON WELL-KNOWN TELEVISION SHOWS.

stereo sound and improved audio quality through both headphones and PC speakers. The company's strong relationship with RealNetworks has been the foundation for this business unit, and provides QSound with an ever increasing customer base for its Internet audio product lines.

The company's technology has been part of the PC/multimedia industry for many years with QSound-enhanced motherboards, codecs, and sound cards. Of special note is QSound's strategic relationship with Philips Electronics, who after several years of co-development, began to market a series of sound cards incorporating QSound technology. The Rhythmic Edge™, Seismic Edge™, and Acoustic Edge™ became available to consumers in 2000. The Acoustic Edge has received critical acclaim from numerous reviewers and has been awarded several Editor's Choice awards.

Computer games by leading developers like Bullfrog Productions, Capcom, Electronic Arts, and Sony Psynosis, and as well as game consoles by Sega, provide consumers with QSound-improved audio, resulting in a more enjoyable computer or gaming experience.

New Direction

In a move aimed at diversification—and based on QSound's own e-commerce experience as a vendor—the company began to focus on the Internet as a vehicle for delivering new e-commerce products and services. After purchasing VirtualSpin, a pioneer in e-commerce site development, QSound formed a wholly owned subsidiary, QCommerce Inc. in order to provide complete e-commerce solutions to small and medium-sized businesses. QCommerce offers a comprehensive portfolio of e-business solutions, including InternetStore™, a complete storefront; affiliateDirect™, an on-line marketing software tool; and the ChoiceMall.com and ChoiceWorld.com shopping portals.

"Retailers will be able to utilize our simple-to-implement solutions to demystify Web commerce, allowing them to build a professional on-line storefront with the same capabilities as larger businesses," says Gallagher.

A Good Location

Calgary is a great place to be headquartered," says Gallagher. "The cost of operating a business is significantly lower than that of our Silicon Valley counterparts, and we generate our revenues in U.S. dollars at world market rates. There is a large talent pool of labour available for high-tech companies locally as a result of the concentration of telecommunications and data processing businesses in the area."

Calgary, of course, is close to the West Coast and convenient to Asia, where many of the company's customers are headquartered. And the center of the entertainment industry, Los Angeles, is only a few hours away. Fans of TV shows such as "The X-Files" can attribute their goose bumps to QSound, even if they're only listening to stereo television.

QSound has positioned itself as a world leader in 3D audio solutions and is poised to take advantage of this leadership position in the coming years. As well, the company's e-commerce investment positions it to take advantage of the fastest-growing sector of the economy: small and medium-sized businesses.

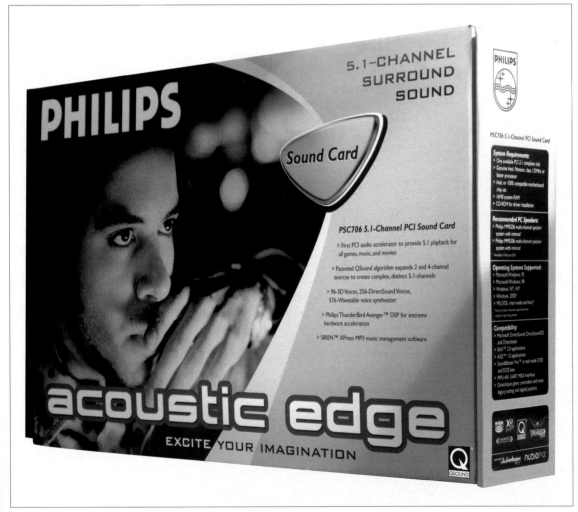

QSOUND'S 3D AUDIO TECHNOLOGY IS CURRENTLY BEING INCLUDED IN PC/MULTIMEDIA CONSUMER ELECTRONICS, INTERNET AUDIO, AND HEALTH CARE PRODUCTS THROUGHOUT THE WORLD.

Trico Homes Inc.

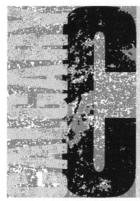

Calgary is truly a land of opportunity for entrepreneurs such as Wayne Chiu, a mechanical engineer by profession. Chiu's interest in real estate investments began in the volatile market of the 1980s. As he became increasingly involved in buying, selling, and managing properties, it was a natural progression to move into home building. ♦ In the early years, Trico Homes Inc. was a small company—with only two employees and contracted professional tradespeople, and a focus on multifamily dwellings. In 1993, Chiu decided to add single-family homes to the company's portfolio. In that year, the company built 12 single-family homes.

A major milestone was reached a few years later when Trico was given the honour of becoming a Parade of Homes builder for one of Calgary's new master-planned communities. By 2000 Trico was building some 150 single-family and estate homes per year, as well as building about 150 condominium units and doing some commercial development. Along the way Chiu received his professional designation as a Master Home Builder.

▼ JOHN JACOBFI

WAYNE CHIU AND HIS ASSOCIATES AT TRICO HOMES INC. HAVE PLEDGED A $500,000 DONATION TO THE KIDS CANCER CARE FOUNDATION OF ALBERTA.

Smart Growth

There are now more than 25 full-time employees at Trico, along with many other contract workers. "We hire a lot of New Canadians," Chiu says. "I believe it's important to provide opportunities for people who want to work hard and make a new life for themselves and their families. Our vision is to combine human and environmental values with financial and business practices, designing and producing fine homes while providing opportunities for staff development and personal rewards."

Since the company was founded, Trico has built more than 1,500 residential units in Calgary, Banff, Okotoks, and Lake Chestermere. The company has targeted both new and established communities, including Royal Oak Estates, Scenic Acres, Varsity Estates, Cimarron in Okotoks, the Lake at Heritage Pointe, WestCreek at Lake Chestermere, Martha's Haven, Saddle Ridge, Hillside Estates, and Hanson Ranch Estates. In addition, the Riverfront, a low-rise condominium project on the Bow River, has significantly impacted lifestyle options for those wishing to live and work downtown. "We build everywhere families want to live," says Chiu.

Trico builds the types of homes people want. There are Trico homes for all kinds of Calgarians, including singles, young couples, young families starting out, middle-aged families upgrading, and empty nesters.

Structurally Sound, Visually Appealing

With a number of engineers employed at Trico, purchasers can be assured that their new homes are structurally sound. But that's only the beginning. Trico has proved itself to be a premier Calgary builder, concerned about both quality and customer care. Every Trico home is built with attention to detail and superb project management from start to finish. Customer satisfaction continues even after the purchaser has moved into the new home, as Trico ensures that any warranty work required is taken care of promptly.

"We know it takes more than a work crew to build a home," says Chiu. "It takes skilled craftspeople, dedicated tradespeople, and honest, caring staff to create every beautiful Trico home."

A member of the Calgary Regional Home Builders Association, Alberta New

"WE KNOW IT TAKES MORE THAN A WORK CREW TO BUILD A HOME," SAYS WAYNE CHIU. "IT TAKES SKILLED CRAFTSPEOPLE, DEDICATED TRADESPEOPLE, AND HONEST, CARING STAFF TO CREATE EVERY BEAUTIFUL TRICO HOME."

Home Warranty Program, and National New Home Warranty Program, Trico demonstrates a sensitivity to the wants and needs of new home-owners. The company's success and continuing growth has, in part, been a result of customer referrals. Another contributor to the company's success has been Chiu's expertise in reading market conditions and coming up with a product that meets customers' needs. He has become known for his marketing analysis and creativity in both project and financial management.

Chiu believes that building homes is basically a management function, requiring appropriate processes to take place at the right time. His engineering training helps ensure that all phases of development and construction run smoothly—from concept and

feasibility studies to detailed design and planning, and timely execution, all combined with after-sales service.

Trico has received recognition from its peers in the construction industry. In 1999, the Alberta Home Builders' Association named Trico an Award of Excellence finalist for its Hanson Creek Manors condominium project.

A Valuable Investment

Trico customers get the best value for their investment. That means that a show home is presented as close to the expected purchase price as possible. There are builders who add a number of upgrades in their show homes, so purchasers cannot buy what they actually see without paying for those extra options.

"Home purchasers see the options in the show homes and don't realize they can add as much as an extra $40,000 to the price of the houses, so we make sure there are only minimal extras in our show homes," notes Chiu. "Such integrity and honesty is very much appreciated by our customers."

Chiu is determined to give back to Calgary—to the community that has made his company's success possible. He has pledged a $100,000 annual contribution for five years to the Kids Cancer Care Foundation of Alberta. In addition, the company contributes financially to training programs for young people entering the construction industry.

Adept at building both single- and multi-family dwellings, Trico's memorable advertising campaign says it all: "Don't worry. Be happy."

TRICO HAS BUILT MORE THAN 1,500 RESIDENTIAL UNITS IN CALGARY, BANFF, OKOTOKS, AND LAKE CHESTERMERE. THERE ARE TRICO HOMES FOR ALL KINDS OF CALGARIANS, INCLUDING SINGLES, YOUNG COUPLES, YOUNG FAMILIES STARTING OUT, MIDDLE-AGED FAMILIES UPGRADING, AND EMPTY NESTERS.

The Calgary Sun

Bucking trends, though a rare practice among media organizations, is among the specialties of The Sun newspaper group. In an era of downsizing and consolidation, the group's cheeky and irreverent tabloid style has beaten the odds. It has been successful in attracting an increasing number of readers and advertisers since the first Sun newspaper started up in the 1970s in Toronto, following the demise of the *Toronto Telegraph*. Next came the

Edmonton version. Then, in 1980, *The Calgary Sun* began with the purchase of the former *Albertan,* and has never looked back.

The Calgary Sun and its counterparts across Canada are now owned by Sun Media Corporation, a Montreal-based Quebecor company. Quebecor is the largest commercial printer in the world and the second-largest newspaper publisher in Canada.

"We weren't given much hope of success in the beginning," says Editor-in-Chief Chris Nelson. "But we proved everyone wrong. People actually read our newspaper, so ad campaigns have a bigger impact and better response, in comparison to our competition."

A Local Newspaper with an Attitude

The Calgary Sun's staff prides itself on producing a local newspaper that focuses its irreverent style on entertainment, local news, and sports. Originally published six days a week, the paper added a Saturday edition on September 17, 1994, and in six short years, readership for the Saturday edition was 186,600 in 2000. Readership of the weekday *Sun* was 234,400 in 2000, while the Sunday *Sun* had a readership of more than 225,600 in 2000. According to Nelson, the *Sun* often gets passed around in coffee shops and waiting rooms, so readership is higher than circulation numbers would indicate.

The Calgary Sun, OWNED BY SUN MEDIA CORPORATION, IS A LOCAL PAPER THAT FOCUSES ITS IRREVERENT STYLE ON ENTERTAINMENT, LOCAL NEWS, AND SPORTS.

"The content and quality of our editorial coverage have been getting progressively better over the years," says Nelson. "We try to mirror the political and social attitudes and philosophy of Calgarians, but we also encourage our columnists to express their own opinions if they are different from ours. Some of our best reporters joined us when they were in their early 20s. They've matured and grown up with the newspaper, and now are among the field's top professionals."

The *Sun* has also matured and grown up with Calgary. When the paper first started, typical readers were single males, which reflected the demographics in Calgary at the time. Now a much higher percentage of readers are female, and most of the male readers are family men, as the demographics of the city have shifted.

Compared to the Calgary newspaper market, daily *Sun* readers—with an average age of 39—tend to be more active, attend more leisure activities, purchase as much or more consumer goods, access the Internet more, are more likely to invest, and have taken more overnight vacation trips. More than 77 percent of readers are currently employed, with an average household income of more than $71,297.

The *Sun* has always played an active role in helping Calgarians in charitable events throughout the community. Almost $1.5 million has been raised through the *Sun*'s Christmas campaign, known as the SunShine Fund, and more than 150 families receive Christmas food and toy hampers every year through the *Sun*'s Adopt-a-Family campaign.

"We sometimes cause a stir and that's good," says Nelson. "We try to give people something to talk about. It's been a winning formula for us for more than 20 years, and we expect that success to continue for decades to come."

Profiles in Excellence

1990

2001

WDC Mackenzie Distributors Limited

he love of golf has led to exciting new careers and a successful partnership for Ryan Magnussen, David Brown, and Vance Mackenzie. "We all wanted to be in the golf business," notes Magnussen, former banker and now President of WDC Mackenzie Distributors Ltd. "Over a beer in 1992, we decided to start a company to sell golfing equipment. During our first year, we worked as an agent, selling products for a number of golf equipment suppliers in the United States. Eventually, we realized that the only way to create a successful company was to obtain the Canadian distribution rights for representing the products."

VANCE MACKENZIE, RYAN MAGNUSSEN, AND DAVID BROWN FOUNDED WDC MACKENZIE DISTRIBUTORS LIMITED IN 1992 (RIGHT).

WHILE SOFTSPIKES BRAND CLEATS STILL ACCOUNT FOR A SIGNIFICANT PORTION OF WDC MACKENZIE'S REVENUES, OTHER PRODUCTS HAVE BEEN ADDED TO THE LINEUP, SUCH AS THE ADAMS GOLF INC. LINE OF GOLF CLUBS, ADAMS' WOODS (TIGHT LIES), BURTON GOLF BAGS, SRIXON GOLF BALLS, AND OTHER LEADING-EDGE GOLFING ITEMS.

Revolutionizing Golf Footwear

When Vance Mackenzie returned from a U.S. trip in 1993 with Softspikes, WDC Mackenzie hit the jackpot. At that time, all golfers wore metal cleats on the greens, even though they damaged the grass and were not particularly comfortable to wear. Softspikes were revolutionary cleats made from plastic, which did not damage the greens and were extremely comfortable.

To market the product, the partners would visit golf courses in the early morning and offer to insert Softspikes on all the golfers' shoes; by day's end, the difference could be easily seen. The partners were also involved in encouraging golf courses to ban metal cleats. These initiatives proved so successful that metal cleats are now only a memory for manufacturers, and Softspikes brand cleats are the Kleenex of the golf world—the brand name most associated with plastic cleats.

While Softspikes brand cleats still account for a significant portion of the company's revenues—about 25 percent—other products have been added to the lineup, including a corporate division to sell promotional products.

In addition to Softspikes, the company's wholesale division sells the well-respected Adams Golf Inc. line of golf clubs. Adams' woods (Tight Lies) offer a unique patented design that promises superior performance. Other major products in the company's wholesale division include Burton golf bags and Srixon golf balls.

WDC Mackenzie has relationships with contracted agents across Canada who sell the company's product lines to golf stores and pro shops. In addition, a telemarketing centre in the Calgary office works with these field representatives to provide follow-up with clients across the country. "It's unusual to have a support system like this, and our clients really appreciate the extra attention they receive," says Magnussen.

Corporate Division Focuses on Promotional Items

Operated totally separately from the distribution business, WDC Mackenzie's corporate division provides a wide range of promotional

products to corporate clients in the Calgary area. The company has developed a range of active wear for the City of Calgary Fire Department, and has provided a unique cedar box within which the Detroit Tigers deliver season tickets. Other popular items include sportswear, outerwear, awards, and incentives. If a client wishes to pro- mote its business, WDC can provide the products and the creative expertise.

"In this line of business, most companies use the same suppliers, so we need to distinguish ourselves by meeting delivery times and by our overall sales service," Magnussen says. "We will do what is necessary to deliver orders on time, and we get verification with our suppliers before we promise anything to our clients."

The firm's corporate division ensures customer satisfaction by offering all the top brands of promotional products, along with leading-edge golfing items. In addition, as a member of Promotional Products Association International, the company has access to more than 30,000 suppliers in North America, as well as exclusive access to a number of unique clothing lines.

"Our corporate division has been growing quickly these past few years, and we are on our way to being one of the best in the business," notes Magnussen.

Growth and Promise

We were fortunate to obtain the distribution rights for some unique products, and they boomed," says Magnussen. Growth has been so rapid that, in 1999, the company was named the 11th-fastest-growing company in Canada by *Profit 100: The Magazine for Canadian Entrepreneurs.* Revenues of the company went from $130,000 in 1993 to $6 million in 1998, an increase of some 4,500 percent.

The partners aren't resting on their laurels, but are planning for the future. While the golf industry is still growing, WDC Mackenzie is focusing on diversification to help offset the seasonal nature of the business. One new product line is Xpress Air, a condensed aerosol can of air that can be used for a number of purposes, such as filling tires, filling or topping off sport balls, and repairing flat tires.

With a focus on diversified products and quality customer service, the company shows great potential. If past success can predict the future, then WDC Mackenzie Distributors is poised for expansion and excellence.

WDC MACKENZIE HAS RELATIONSHIPS WITH CONTRACTED AGENTS ACROSS CANADA WHO SELL THE COMPANY'S PRODUCT LINES TO GOLF STORES AND PRO SHOPS.

WHILE THE GOLF INDUSTRY IS STILL GROWING, WDC MACKENZIE IS FOCUSING ON DIVERSIFICATION TO HELP OFFSET THE SEASONAL NATURE OF THE BUSINESS.

Cisco Systems
Canada Co.

California-based Cisco Systems is a worldwide leader in networking for the Internet. Cisco's networking solutions connect people, computing devices, and computer networks, allowing users to access or transfer information without regard to differences in time, place, or type of computer system. Cisco serves customers in three target markets: enterprises; service providers such as telecommunications and Internet providers; and small to medium-

sized businesses. Enterprises are large organizations with complex networking needs, usually spanning multiple locations and types of computer systems. Enterprise customers include corporations, government agencies, utilities, and educational institutions.

The company established its Calgary presence–Cisco Systems Canada Co.–in 1993, with the intention of augmenting the company's enterprise business in western Canada. "We see Calgary as a high-growth opportunity," says Gilles St. Hilaire, manager, western region, Enterprise Operations. "Calgary is becoming a high-tech centre, and there are lots of large oil and gas companies with their headquarters located here."

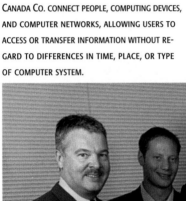

THE NETWORKING SOLUTIONS OF CISCO SYSTEMS CANADA CO. CONNECT PEOPLE, COMPUTING DEVICES, AND COMPUTER NETWORKS, ALLOWING USERS TO ACCESS OR TRANSFER INFORMATION WITHOUT RE-GARD TO DIFFERENCES IN TIME, PLACE, OR TYPE OF COMPUTER SYSTEM.

Innovative Networking Solutions

Cisco has evolved over the past decade from selling products to developing solutions and ultimately to serving as trusted advisers to clients. The company provides end-to-end networking solutions to help customers build a unified information infrastructure of their own, or to connect to someone else's network. An end-to-end networking solution provides a common architecture that delivers consistent network services to all users. The broader the range of network services, the more capabilities a network can provide to users connected to it.

Cisco offers the industry's broadest range of hardware products used to form information networks or give users access to those networks. Cisco IOS® software provides network services and enables networked applications. The company also offers expertise in network design and implementation, as well as technical support and professional services to maintain and optimize network operations.

"We're unique in our ability to provide all these elements, either by ourselves or together with partners," says St. Hilaire. "Everybody who uses a computer, even to send e-mail over the Internet, is using a Cisco product, either directly or indirectly."

A strong emphasis is also placed on satisfying customers, which can be seen in the company's slogan, "the network works–no excuses!" Cisco's operations philosophy comprises listening to customer requests, monitoring all technological alternatives, and providing customers with a range of options from which to choose.

Global Networked Business Model

Every day, Cisco and its customers are proving that networking and the Internet can fundamentally and profitably change the way companies do business. Cisco describes this change as the Global Networked Business model. A Global Networked Business is an enterprise, of any size, that strategically uses informa-

tion and communications to build a network of vital, interactive relationships with its key constituencies.

The Global Networked Business model leverages the network for competitive advantage by opening up the corporate information infrastructure to all key constituencies. The model employs a self-help model of information access that is more efficient and responsive than the traditional model of an information gatekeeper dispensing the data.

Cisco itself is a leading example of a Global Networked Business. "Eighty percent of our customers make their purchases over the Internet," says St. Hilaire. "We practise what we preach."

Cisco participates in the Netera Alliance, an Alberta-based, not-for-profit alliance of companies and institutions promoting the development of information infrastructure in the province. Established in 1993 as WurcNet, the alliance built the first regional advanced network in Canada, and continues to design and manage the Advanced Internet in Alberta.

Learning Opportunities

A strong commitment to empowering the Internet generation led Cisco to develop its unique Networking Academy. The Networking Academy is based on a cooperative partnership between school boards, community colleges, and Cisco Systems Canada. The program pairs schools with private industry to give thousands of students across Canada the opportunity to learn some of the networking and information technology (IT) skills needed to be successful in the information economy. A complete, four-semester, hands-on course on the principles and practice of designing, building, and maintaining networks for national and global organizations is offered.

"This is the shop class of the new century," says St. Hilaire. "We also personally speak to graduating classes about where and how to look for jobs in the industry. The Networking Academy helps prepare students for the Cisco Certified Networking Associate exam, and qualifies them for building and maintaining networks."

The Networking Academy program is customized to meet the individual needs of high schools and colleges. The program is available in 215 Canadian schools, reaching more than 3,000 students. In Alberta, six schools now offer the program, including the Northern and Southern Institutes of Technology, and high schools in Calgary, Edmonton, High River, Sherwood Park, and Pincher Creek.

Graduates of the program are well prepared to meet the needs of their employers. The Alberta government has indicated that the number of information communication technologists (ICT) in the province must double to meet the industry's growing demand. Some 60 percent of all ICT jobs are on the networking side of the business.

Increasingly, network decisions will be a key factor in the success or failure of businesses. Since shipping its first product in 1986, Cisco has grown into a global market leader that holds first or second place in virtually every market segment in which it participates. It is obvious that the company has and will continue to set the standard for networks throughout the world.

CISCO'S NETWORKING ACADEMY PAIRS SCHOOLS WITH PRIVATE INDUSTRY TO GIVE THOUSANDS OF STUDENTS ACROSS CANADA THE OPPORTUNITY TO LEARN SOME OF THE NETWORKING AND INFORMATION TECHNOLOGY (IT) SKILLS THEY WILL NEED TO BE SUCCESSFUL IN THE INFORMATION ECONOMY.

EVERY DAY, CISCO AND ITS CUSTOMERS ARE PROVING THAT NETWORKING AND THE INTERNET CAN FUNDAMENTALLY AND PROFITABLY CHANGE THE WAY COMPANIES DO BUSINESS.

Crape Geomatics Corporation

Specializing in field surveying, land mapping, and land information services, Crape Geomatics Corporation has doubled its sales almost every year since its founding in 1993. Crape clients, along with many others, believe the company is well on its way to ranking in the top five survey companies in Alberta. ❧ "We're driven by client feedback," says Mike Crape, founder and President. "We don't create a service and make the clients fit the service.

We learn to ask–not tell–clients what they need, and we spend a significant amount of time at the front end constructing research and establishing a good understanding of the client's situation."

The company's commitment to service has paid off in a few short years. Currently undertaking 1,000 to 1,500 projects every year, Crape Geomatics must turn down projects routinely to ensure the company doesn't overextend itself. The firm's success is achieved with little active marketing– acquiring most of its clients through referrals.

Adding a Partner to Support Growth

A major milestone in Crape Geomatics' history was bringing co-owner Jim MacLeod on board in January 1996.

"For the first three years, I didn't have a day off," says Crape. "There were lots of opportunities, but I couldn't pursue them on my own. I had worked with Jim before, and I knew he was a very good operations person, so he came on as general manager. Now I focus just on the corporate, financial,

and business development needs of the company. We're very clear about our roles, so we have a strong working relationship."

Another major milestone was a name change in 1999. The name Crape Land Surveys no longer reflected the full scope of the company's activities. The new name, Crape Geomatics, better depicts the broad range of disciplines the company uses to create detailed, understandable images of the physical world.

Crape Geomatics now employs a core of some 90 field and office staff. The company's head office is located in Calgary, with field crews dispatched from seven strategic hubs throughout the province. In addition to core activities in Alberta and Saskatchewan, Crape has experience in resource-related surveys in Russia, South America, and northern Canada. The firm's clients include large companies such as Rogers AT&T, PanCanadian Petroleum, Anadarko Canada, and Crestar Energy, as well as a number of smaller companies.

Typical projects include field surveys for well-site, pipeline, and oil and gas production facilities, as well as for road construc-

tion and new subdivisions. Typical digital mapping services consist of computer-aided drafting, composite maps, and aerial maps. Land information services include access to land titles, regulatory records, maps, and other data.

JIM MACLEOD (LEFT) AND MIKE CRAPE, CO-OWNERS OF CRAPE GEOMATICS CORPORATION, ARE CLEAR ABOUT THEIR ROLES—UNDERSTANDING THE NEEDS OF EVERY CLIENT AND DELIVERING EFFICIENT, DIGITAL SOLUTIONS THAT COMPLEMENT THOSE NEEDS (TOP).

WITH MORE THAN 90 EMPLOYEES ON STAFF, CRAPE GEOMATICS STRONGLY BELIEVES THAT CREATING A FUN, RELAXED ENVIRONMENT IS ESSENTIAL TO THE OVERALL SUCCESS OF THE COMPANY (BOTTOM).

Technology Cuts Turnaround Time

In addition to always meeting clients' needs, Crape Geomatics is dedicated to faster turnaround times. Delivering electronic services since its founding, Crape remains the only fully digital survey company of its kind in Calgary.

Field staff collect data with electronic data collectors and e-mail the information to the head office daily for processing and drafting–providing major benefits to clients. Turnaround time is reduced substantially, delivering an end product that is often better than that produced through conventional means. Additionally, both field and office work can proceed in a parallel, rather a sequential, manner.

"In addition to the phenomenal turnaround time, we can address any field problem right away, rather than waiting for the completion of data collection," says Crape.

Yet another advantage at Crape Geomatics is its staff. Crape's highly qualified and efficient employees bring a broad range of experience from all aspects of the oil and gas industry.

"We have a team that's out of this world," says Crape. "Personality is important, and when we hire new people, we make sure they fit in with our culture."

As Crape Geomatics continues to grow, hiring remains a strong focus. The company routinely visits schools across Canada to seek out new graduates–hiring 12 graduates from post-secondary schools across Canada in 2000.

The Right Employee Has Community Spirit

To successfully attract the right kinds of employees, Crape Geomatics has undertaken an awareness campaign that commenced when the company name changed. Focused on community, one highlight of the 2000 awareness program involved the company's sponsorship of a chuckwagon and driver at the Calgary Stampede. Appearing at this premier event, the Crape Geomatics chuckwagon made the circuit of all races in the province–competing in rodeos in Medicine Hat, High River, Grande Prairie, Calgary, and Strathmore, to name a few.

Honesty and Integrity Paves the Way

Ultimately, Crape Geomatics' mission is to provide fast, accurate digital solutions and prompt, flexible, personalized service.

"We work hard to keep our products honest," says Crape. "And we believe that when people do good work every day, the future takes care of itself."

CRAPE'S MANAGEMENT TEAM DELIVERS A VALUABLE COMBINATION OF EXPERTISE, HONESTY, AND INTEGRITY–A DRIVING FORCE THAT CONSISTENTLY PAVES THE WAY TO ITS SUCCESS.

THE CRAPE GEOMATICS CHUCKWAGON, FEATURING RENOWNED DRIVER TYLER HELMIG, IS ONE OF THE MANY WAYS THE COMPANY DEMONSTRATES ITS COMMITMENT TO ALBERTA'S HERITAGE.

Cybersurf Corporation

stablished in Calgary, Cybersurf Corporation is an Internet technology company in the business of developing and marketing innovative software, connectivity, multimedia, and communications solutions. On August 4, 1998, Calgary-based Cybersurf launched the world's first free Internet service supported by a proprietary desktop advertising component, and the company has never looked back. According to President and CEO Paul Mercia, the 3web Network is the

company's crown jewel and stands as testimony that Calgary is indeed becoming a player in the information technology game.

Founded by Mercia in 1994, Cybersurf's focus has always been Internet technology. Cybersurf was the first company in the world to develop Internet banking and network computing software, but these technologies were never aggressively marketed outside of Calgary. It wasn't until the 3web Network was launched that the company started to receive national attention for its free Internet service. Subsequently, Cybersurf has received interest from the international marketplace in its Internet and new media technologies.

Focus on Internet

ounded on September 24, 1994, Cybersurf went public and was listed on the Alberta Stock Exchange (ASE), under the symbol CY, in December 1995. In 1996, the company completed its first major transaction on the ASE. In 1997, Cybersurf purchased Dognet Communications Corp., a value-added reseller of LAN/WAN products and telecommunications services in western Canada. This acquisition represented the next step in the diversification of

Cybersurf into LAN/WAN networking and "Internetworking" solutions, dial-up Internet services, and Internet software development.

Following four years of development, the 3web Network version 1.1 was officially launched in August 1998, offering all residents of Calgary free, unlimited Internet and E-mail access. Then, in early 1999, Cybersurf

launched its on-line auction service, 3auction, a joint venture with Alberta's largest auction house, Graham Auctions. Designed as a value-added component of the 3web Network, 3auction offers a wide variety of goods and services for 3web users to bid on, as well as an area where individuals can place items up for auction.

CYBERSURF

DEVELOPING COMMUNICATIONS SOLUTIONS
THROUGH VISION, TALENT AND TECHNOLOGY

BASED IN CALGARY, CYBERSURF CORPORATION IS AN INTERNET TECHNOLOGY COMPANY IN THE BUSINESS OF DEVELOPING AND MARKETING INNOVATIVE SOFTWARE, CONNECTIVITY, MULTIMEDIA, AND COMMUNICATIONS SOLUTIONS.

Following the introduction of 3auction, Cybersurf's growth began to accelerate. In March 1999, the 3web Network was launched in its second city—Edmonton—to overwhelming public response. In November, Toronto was added, and an office was established there to take care of advertising sales and corporate development. Early April 2000 saw Vancouver become the fourth city to offer 3web.

To achieve this level of success, the company has had to obtain financing. The ease with which this has been accomplished provides another measure of Cybersurf's success. In mid-1999, the firm was able to raise $25 million in only six days. In fact, the offer was well oversubscribed.

3web

ike many other free services, 3web is based on advertiser support. However, Cybersurf's Sprite animation technology makes 3web unique and provides an added competitive advantage: advertisers can directly cross-purpose existing television commercials into 3web's medium, maintaining the integrity of the original creation. This allows 3web's advertising clients to maximize the value from their expensive investments in TV production, while gaining further market penetration with consumers.

"The Sprite technology, which was completely developed in-house, is what is referred to as a rich medium," says Mercia. "It enables us to create ads with fluid motion, full stereo sound, and even intelligent text, such as the user's name. Other Internet service providers can only deliver ads in the form of static images, or crude, looping animations without sound. We're all familiar with banner ads; they're like billboards. Ads like that only achieve a 0.35 percent response rate from consumers. Our ads, which look and sound just like TV commercials, average about an 8 percent response rate, at no additional cost to advertisers."

That phenomenal response rate is due to many factors. Each 3web subscriber completes a personal profile when he or she signs up for the service, providing demographic and psychographic information that allows the ads to target specific types of individuals. Furthermore, each ad appears in a box on a smart advertising bar that is separated from the user's Internet browser. Although subscribers can move the box ads around on their screen, it remains on top of the browser as long as it's open—even on top of other applications if they're being used. Therefore, exposure is guaranteed.

In addition, 3web advertisers can determine exactly how many hits their ads receive. They also have access to a wealth of informa-

tion about each subscriber who responds to their ads, including his or her complete demographic profile. This is one of 3web's most attractive features from an advertiser's perspective. Big-name advertisers continue to jump on the 3web bandwagon, including Labatts, Molson, Indigo, Husky, IBM, Procter & Gamble, Unilever, and many more.

Unique Marketing Efforts in Canada

ith 3web, Cybersurf is poised to capture a substantial share of the Internet advertising market in Canada and North America. 3web, according to Mercia, is easily the number one name in Canada for free Internet access: "We have more than 10 times the number of subscribers of any other free Internet service provider," he says. "The others came into the market late, following in our footsteps. They don't have our market share, and they don't have our Sprite technology. Many times the service they offer is inferior, and they are trying to attract advertising dollars with banner ads."

In the near future, Cybersurf anticipates having a total of more than 1 million 3web subscribers in Calgary, Edmonton, Toronto, and Vancouver. The company currently is planning national penetration of its service, and ultimately intends to market its unique technology on a global level.

FOUNDER, PRESIDENT, AND CEO PAUL MERCIA AIMS TO MAKE CYBERSURF'S NAME SYNONYMOUS WITH INNOVATION.

LIKE MANY OTHER FREE SERVICES, 3WEB IS BASED ON ADVERTISER SUPPORT. HOWEVER, CYBERSURF'S SPRITE ANIMATION TECHNOLOGY MAKES 3WEB UNIQUE AND PROVIDES AN ADDED COMPETITIVE ADVANTAGE: ADVERTISERS CAN DIRECTLY CROSS-PURPOSE EXISTING TELEVISION COMMERCIALS INTO 3WEB'S MEDIUM, MAINTAINING THE INTEGRITY OF THE ORIGINAL CREATIVE.

Cybersurf's marketing efforts have been as innovative as its Internet efforts. In Toronto and Vancouver, 3web is being marketed and distributed through Petro-Canada locations. In addition, the company signed a strategic alliance agreement with HMV in March 2000. This agreement will introduce free Internet and e-mail services to tens of thousands of HMV customers in Canada, and will significantly increase the 3web subscriber base. The HMV 3web installation CDs are being sold for a nominal fee—to cover the cost of CD production—at participating HMV retail outlets.

"Working together, we believe that each company can use the other's assets and core competencies to their own advantage," says Mercia. " The deal we've struck with HMV, for example, will help us to achieve our goal of 1 million users, but will also solidify their position as a leading Internet retailer."

Poised to Take on the World

Cybersurf recently developed a Spanish-language version of 3web for Latin America and Spain, and has signed software licensing agreements with Latin American, U.S., and Asian firms. A Cantonese-language version of 3web is currently in development at Cybersurf. The company is also focusing on creating and marketing the peripheral products of the 3web Network, including the 3web Galleria, an e-commerce-driven online shopping mall; 3auction, a licensed on-line auction service; and business-to-business Internet communication along with its now Web-enabled Sprite animation technology.

Like many products within the information technology arena, timing has been critical to 3web's survival. Cybersurf's 3web Network has achieved phenomenal success in a relatively short period of time, largely due to the Internet's growth and to increased public accessibility. There are now more than 85 employees in the company's Calgary and Toronto offices, with "a new face every day," according to Mercia.

Mercia is certainly one of the visionary and driving forces behind 3web's success. "I believe there will one day be a box in the corner of every house," he says. "This box will walk and talk, and manage all the functions of the house and its communications systems. We'll need to take a bunch of baby steps to achieve that vision, and 3web is one of those baby steps."

New Media and Internet Services

Cybersurf provides a wide range of software development, Internet, and new media services to its clients in Calgary and Toronto. Its digital communications division, Interactive Media, develops integrated, solution-based communications tools such as Web sites and interactive presentations for a variety of client

CYBERSURF ANTICIPATES HAVING A TOTAL OF MORE THAN 1 MILLION 3WEB SUBSCRIBERS IN CALGARY, EDMONTON, TORONTO, AND VANCOUVER. THE COMPANY ULTIMATELY INTENDS TO MARKET ITS UNIQUE TECHNOLOGY ON A GLOBAL LEVEL.

companies. This division carries out all advertising creation for the 3web Network as well. The core competencies of Interactive Media include corporate communications, advertising design, print collateral, digital imaging, Web site design, CD-ROM authoring, three-D modeling, and computer animation.

The 3web project was created entirely in-house by Cybersurf's Software Development division. This team also develops a variety of software applications for client companies, ranging from simple data base projects to entire market-ready software applications, such as Coachware Hockey. Because the company has an extensive in-house programming division, from HTML to more advanced languages such as Delphi, Cybersurf has the unique ability to develop and maintain its internal projects, such as the 3web Network, and to create all manner of software and Web-based applications for its clients.

Cybersurf's Internetworking division provides residential to business-level network solutions, including dial-up Internet service with fast, reliable, and efficient connections on digital modems. Clients can select a package to suit their specific needs.

Cybersurf Internetworking also offers Web hosting services for clients looking for an inexpensive way to make their mark on the Internet. The company also has a secu-rity specialist on staff to help clients add the right amount of firewall protection to their networks, with a variety of options including the company's own Cyberwall. Cybersurf also provides security audits and can even help write clients' initial security policy. The company provides end-to-end advanced digital subscriber line (ADSL) support in the city of Calgary, wireless connectivity solutions, and virtual private networks.

Inside Talent

Cybersurf is staffed by a team of young, dedicated software developers and new media designers who have spent the last several years creating the 3web Network, and are now aggressively marketing their services to the information technology marketplace. Their mission is an ambitious and challenging one: "To strive to create the best Internet service in North America supported by the best animation and advertising technology in the world."

The talent of its software developers and multimedia producers has been a major factor in Cybersurf's success. "They're an innovative, entrepreneurial crew who act like they're running their own business," notes Mercia. "They feel like they're part of the direction of the company, and they're right."

Unusual for a high-tech company, there has been zero staff turnover since the company first started operations, although salaries are not the highest in the industry. Obviously, Cybersurf is a great place to work.

And Mercia notes that Calgary is a great place to live. It has a culture that fosters innovation and entrepreneurship. The city is the perfect size for the company, and its proximity to the mountains offers some unique opportunities. "We take advantage of our wonderful location, and often go to the mountains on retreats to help us brainstorm and come up with new ideas," says Mercia.

From the first patented network computer and the world's first on-line banking software, to the world's first advertisement-driven free Internet and e-mail service, all of the company's products began with a unique insight into the possibilities of technology. Through planning, effort, and a network of alliances, Cybersurf has put its innovation to work for thousands of people. The company's mandate is simple, yet salient: developing communications solutions through vision, talent, and technology. By striving steadfastly toward this mission, Cybersurf has made its name synonymous with innovation.

WITH 3WEB, CYBERSURF IS POISED TO CAPTURE A SUBSTANTIAL SHARE OF THE INTERNET ADVERTISING MARKET IN CANADA AND NORTH AMERICA.

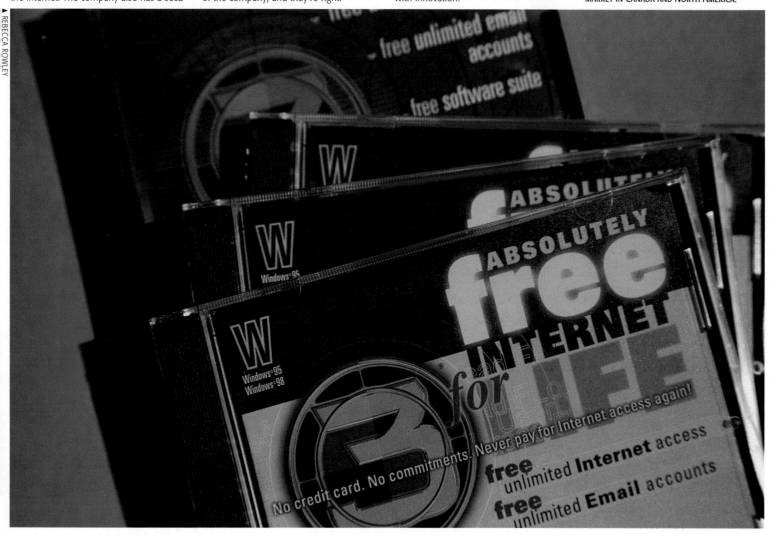

Remington Development Corporation

Calgary-based Remington Development Corporation is a major developer of commercial, retail, warehouse, and office properties. The company is locally owned by three partners who have more than 80 years of combined experience in all aspects of property development. ◆ Remington was founded in 1994 by Randy Remington, Chairman. Partners Larry Mason, President, and Helmut Ebinger, Construction Manager and Vice President,

bring a wealth of experience to the table. Each of the three partners has experience in planning, financing, leasing, budgeting, designing, supervising, and managing construction projects.

In addition to constructing and managing its own properties, Remington constructs and manages buildings for the investment community, including pension funds and life insurance companies. The company also provides a complete range of services, such as site assessment and evaluation, permits and approvals, interior design and space planning, construction, architecture, engineering, occupancy requirements, and property management.

A Premier Developer

he company is becoming known for its ability to develop innovative solutions that benefit a wide range of stakeholders—from corporations to investors and municipal governments. The company's joint venture with the City of Calgary is a case in point. On Remington's initiative, the company provided servicing for a parcel of city-owned land in the Deerfoot Business Park in northeast Calgary. As a result, the city was able to bring commercial land on-stream far earlier than it would have otherwise.

One of the factors making Remington a unique company is the direct involvement of the partners in every property owned or under development. "It's a mandate of this company to maintain a scale of operation that allows clients to deal directly with the principals," says Mason. "The partners are involved in making every decision—we're in touch every day and every hour, if necessary. Few other companies offer the same degree of intensive, local supervision."

The Remington commitment to excellence is reflected in this hands-on involvement in each project, and in ongoing relationships with owners and tenants long past project completion. Clients have peace of mind knowing they can call at any time if they have a question or problem.

Acting as its own general contractor, Remington has its own project managers and site supervisors working together on each project. By using some of the best subcontractors in the construction industry, the company can deliver quality projects on time and on budget, or even ahead of time and under budget.

"The typical construction process has a contractor, an architect, and an owner all wearing different hats to accomplish different things," says Mason. "We offer a seamless package. We do everything in-house, and it saves time as well as money. We haven't missed a deadline yet."

THE POSITIVE TESTIMONIALS FROM CLIENTS SUCH AS (CLOCKWISE FROM TOP LEFT) SEARS, XEROX, CHEMCRAFT INTERNATIONAL, AND MANY OTHERS ARE PROOF OF REMINGTON DEVELOPMENT CORPORATION'S UNIQUE EXPERTISE.

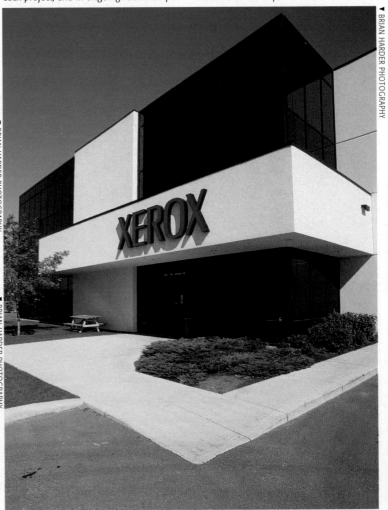

Growing Client Base

While Remington clients take on many forms with varied requirements, they typically are not interested in owning their own facilities and want to rely on outside professionals to provide them with a facility. Although many of the clients are based in Calgary, the company has worked for clients throughout Canada and North America. In addition to its head office in Calgary, the company also maintains an office in Edmonton.

The satisfaction that Remington clients have with the firm's efforts is evidenced by the positive testimonials from company clients such as Movers International, Xerox, Dresser Canada, Minolta, Canada Safeway, Chemcraft International, and Sears. This success has brought Remington a host of new projects. In 2000, the company developed

in excess of 1 million square feet of commercial and industrial property in Calgary—one quarter of the city's total development.

Current projects in 2000-2001 include an Edmonton distribution centre for the United Farmers Association, the Calgary Co-op Shopping Centre in Airdrie, a warehouse facility for USCO, the Portland Street Depot distribution centre, the 52nd Street Business Centre, a design-build project for Geo-X, and the Centre Eight Ten facility in Calgary.

Recognition

Industry peers evidently agree with Remington's satisfied clients, as the company's Deerfoot Distribution Centre was selected by the Building Owners and Managers Association (BOMA) as Building of the Year in 1998 in the multitenant industry professional cat-

egory. The Dresser Canada facility in Calgary was chosen as BOMA's runner-up in the single-tenant category. Glendeer Junction received BOMA recognition as Suburban Office Building of the Year for 1999.

Remington's team has the ability to transform raw materials into long-lasting building solutions. Such expertise has earned Remington a name for the honest way the company does business, as well as for the thoroughness and skill the firm brings to every job, the quality of its people, its products, and its performance. "We don't just give lip service to words like integrity and quality," says Mason. "If we're going to do it, we'll do it right."

REMINGTON'S OFFICES LOCATED AT GLENDEER JUNCTION (LEFT) AND CARMA'S OFFICES (RIGHT) REFLECT THE COMPANY'S COMMITMENT TO EXCELLENCE. IN ADDITION TO ITS HEAD OFFICE IN CALGARY, REMINGTON ALSO MAINTAINS AN OFFICE IN EDMONTON.

IN SOUTHWEST CALGARY, REMINGTON DEVELOPED THE RETAIL CENTRE RICHMOND PLACE.

Hi-Tech Assembly Systems Inc.

Hi-Tech Assembly Systems Inc. was founded in 1995 by Nick Moss, the owner of Alliance Cables. This move helped to establish Calgary as a high-tech centre of excellence. Hi-Tech specializes in manufacturing and supplying wire and cable assemblies for the telecommunications wireless, electronic, and related industries throughout Canada and internationally. Nick Moss, Chairman, continues to provide guidance in strategic planning and global expansion.

The company was founded when Calgary-based Nortel Networks wanted to outsource the function of putting assemblies, or cable connections, together. Many of the Nortel staff working on the cable assemblies at the time of inception made the transition to the new company and are still valued Hi-Tech employees today.

Hi-Tech has not departed from its western communications market tradition; however, the company has undertaken a strategy of diversification, and now has clients across Canada and the United States. Current clients include some of the largest global communication companies and service providers in North America. In a few short years, Hi-Tech

has positioned itself among many of the top cable assembly suppliers.

In 2000 President and Chief Operations Officer Shlomo Brenner came on board to lead the company's growth plan. "Quality is a given," Brenner says. "We pride ourselves in providing excellent service to our customers and building long-term relationships to meet our customers' requirements on a global basis."

Hi-Tech's mission is to provide products and services that conform to the customers' specified requirements through the company's comprehensive total quality management system. The value chain system on which Hi-Tech has based its strategy has been driving its success, with the com-

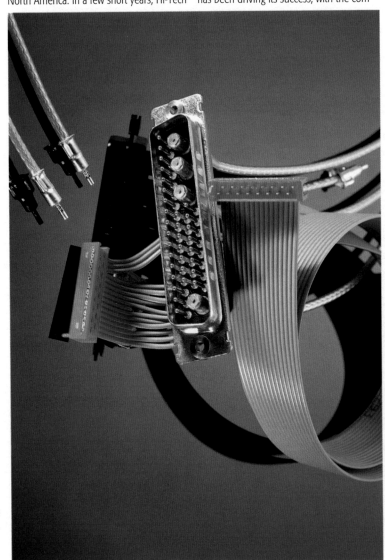

mitment from employees for continuous improvement through preventive and corrective action.

Hi-Tech's product line includes coaxial cable assemblies, data and ribbon cable assemblies, semirigid and delay lines, discrete wire assemblies, and electromechanical contract manufacturing. The product lines include fibre-optic cables, overmoulded assembly, and printed circuit board assemblies.

Globalization

Hi-Tech has entered the new millennium with renewed enthusiasm. "We are striving to move from being a regional supplier to becoming a global one," says Brenner. "We are a young, dynamic company on the way to expanding both our manufacturing capability and the number of our facilities. The Hi-Tech goal, as clearly outlined in our mission statement, is customer satisfaction. All levels of the company, from the head office to the manufacturing floor, are fully committed to this end."

As part of the global expansion strategy to attract a larger share of the cable assembly industry, the company has undertaken a number of joint ventures to diversify its operations. In addition to the company's 30,000-square-foot manufacturing plant in Calgary, Hi-Tech has production plants in Mississauga; Reynosa, Mexico; Greenville, South Carolina; and, most recently, China and Europe.

"Now we can tell customers in those locations that we can build assemblies for them locally, and that is a strategic advantage," says Brenner. "In addition, we offer a complete package based on quality, delivery, service, and price." Hi-Tech is cost-sensitive, always striving to provide the best cost solutions—from start-up to production, as well as year-after-year productivity improvements.

Hi-Tech's commitment to quality is clearly illustrated by its ISO 9001 certification, which guides all aspects of the company's business. In addition, significant capital equipment investments have resulted in state-of-the-art, highly efficient production facilities.

The company's delivery performance is measured at the highest levels by maintaining

HI-TECH ASSEMBLY SYSTEMS INC. SPECIALIZES IN MANUFACTURING AND SUPPLYING WIRE AND CABLE ASSEMBLIES FOR THE TELECOMMUNICATIONS WIRELESS, ELECTRONIC, AND RELATED INDUSTRIES THROUGHOUT CANADA AND INTERNATIONALLY.

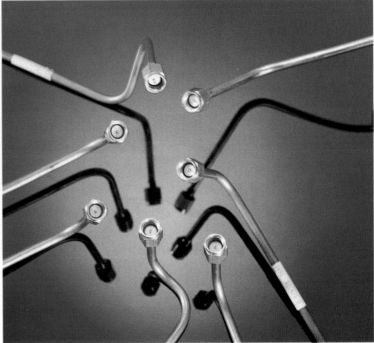

inventory and delivery programs such as supplier-on-site and Kanban systems. Customers' needs are handled quickly and efficiently, with additional flexibility provided by the firm's multiple production locations.

Innovation

n the quest for technical improvement, Hi-Tech's engineering staff provides value-added support for customer design, industry specific testing requirements, and functional design. In addition to ensuring a quality product, testing for continuity, resistance, hi-pot, and insertion loss is standard, while other tests such as phase matching and intermod can be performed if required.

Customers can take advantage of Hi-Tech's policy of offering resources and facilities for new designs and technology improvements. Company designers can develop new product processes for prototypes or custom builds along with full preproduction and first article evaluation report. Hi-Tech also offers, as a standard practice, product recommendations and innovative solutions to meet customers' needs.

Hi-Tech provides its customers with a number of other advantages, as well. The company has global access to components and cable through key channel partners like Alliance Cables. Flexible manufacturing systems and quick response to market needs have made Hi-Tech successful in a very competitive global market.

It always pays to be well connected, according to Hi-Tech Assembly Systems Inc. The company is well on its way to turning its vision into reality—connecting customers to the rest of the world.

HI-TECH'S MISSION IS TO PROVIDE PRODUCTS AND SERVICES THAT CONFORM TO THE CUSTOMERS' SPECIFIED REQUIREMENTS THROUGH THE COMPANY'S COMPREHENSIVE TOTAL QUALITY MANAGEMENT SYSTEM.

HI-TECH'S COMMITMENT TO QUALITY IS CLEARLY ILLUSTRATED BY ITS ISO 9001 CERTIFICATION, WHICH GUIDES ALL ASPECTS OF THE COMPANY'S BUSINESS. IN ADDITION, SIGNIFICANT CAPITAL EQUIPMENT INVESTMENTS HAVE RESULTED IN STATE-OF-THE-ART, HIGHLY EFFICIENT PRODUCTION FACILITIES.

Avmax Group Inc.

vmax Group Inc. was founded in 1996 by a group of well-established professionals actively involved in the aviation industry. A 100 percent Canadian-owned company, Avmax started operations initially with two employees and has quickly grown to more than 140 employees who produce revenues of $3 million per month. ❦ Avmax provides aviation management and support services worldwide to regional and corporate aircraft operators. The business

philosophy of the organization is one that truly focuses on people, relationships, and communication. The people at Avmax have created an environment that, in itself, has attracted customers internationally. Relationships developed through Avmax's environment have provided opportunities that have led to significant growth and diversification into various support services within the aviation industry. Communication is what sustains the company's environment, strengthens its relationships, and denotes Avmax as a leader in aviation management and support services.

Avmax maintains offices in Calgary and Montreal, as well as in Melbourne, Australia. Seventy-five percent of the company's business is international, but Calgary is still home to Avmax's head office. There is an immense amount of aviation expertise in the area,

and Calgary International Airport, which is accessible and well known worldwide, adds strength to Avmax's position in the industry.

Avmax Divisions

he Aircraft Maintenance Organization was the first division of the Avmax Group, and remains the center and forefront of all operations. The division's first customer was air industry giant Bombardier in Montreal, where Avmax commenced doing reconfigurations on new turboprop and jet aircraft destined for operators throughout the world. The facility in Calgary encompasses more than 60,000 square feet of hangar and support shop space, and is strategically located on the airfield in close proximity to many sub-contract support services. In addition to in-

house maintenance, avionics, modification, reconfiguration, and refurbishment services, this division also provides mobile repair teams to support manufacturers and operators throughout the world.

The company's Aviation Support Services division is focused on providing training and line flying support for both manufacturers and operators alike. By providing extensively trained simulator and flight line instructors, Avmax has garnered an excellent reputation in the industry. By providing the resources to carry out initial training on aircraft, followed by flight line support once the crews commence line operations, Avmax lends a seamless transition for operators introducing a new aircraft type. The firm also provides experienced and well-trained flight crews for companies and airlines to supplement existing flight resources. The Aviation Support

AVMAX GROUP INC. IS DEDICATED TO BECOMING A WORLD LEADER IN AVIATION SUPPORT AND MANAGEMENT SERVICES.

Services group offers Web-enabled, computer-based training for pilots, engineers, and flight attendants. In addition, the group provides airline start-up support services, including operations; manual development and publication; and scanning and archival of aircraft critical documents.

Avmax's Spares Management Services group was developed to take advantage of the high returns generated from the sale, lease, and consignment of aftermarket regional aircraft engines and inventories. The facility provides management services such as purchasing and logistical support to major maintenance centers and operators. Additional consignment inventories are managed and sold through this division, allowing operators to centralize their resources and minimize their capital costs, while maintaining reliability.

New Age Thinking

Avmax is dedicated to becoming a world leader in aviation support and management services, and is committed to providing the highest standard of service in a cost-effective environment. The goal is to provide a professional and quality product that exceeds customer expectations. Avmax strives to be the only company in the world that provides all of these services under a single roof.

Avmax's customers appreciate the company's attention to detail, as well as its strict control over budgets and deadlines. With a unique opportunity to obtain all aviation requirements from a single source, customers save time and money by eliminating the need for multiple sourcing.

The never-ending demand for aviation management and support services in all areas of the aviation industry is something that Avmax recognizes. Taking into account this demand, considerable planning and research goes into every program that the company takes on. Avmax recognizes that the strength of the company comes from the people within it, and prides itself on being able to attract entrepreneurial individuals who enable the company to continually bring forward new ideas and process improvements. In addition, Avmax works closely with the Southern Alberta Institute of Technology by offering aeronautical students employment opportunities while they are involved in their courses and after graduation.

Future Plans

Future plans for Avmax include a state-of-the-art, interactive Web site that will allow customers to communicate on a variety of issues, generate requests for qualifications, and track work orders. Pilots and maintenance personnel

will also be able to submit résumés for employment on-line.

Avmax plans to expand its business into the high-growth area of regional airlines in Europe and the Far East. Other areas for possible growth are through the organization's newly created Training and Document Management Services division. Through this division, Avmax will provide technical publications, electronic filing of documents, and on-line training courses.

With its clear goal of becoming a world leader in aviation management and support services, Avmax is truly ready for takeoff.

AT AVMAX, THE GOAL IS TO PROVIDE A PROFESSIONAL AND QUALITY PRODUCT THAT EXCEEDS CUSTOMER EXPECTATIONS.

Dow Chemical Canada Inc.

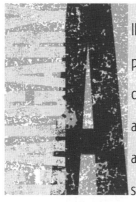

All around the world, people depend on The Dow Chemical Company. From polyester fibres for clothing to shaving cream, from garden hoses to shower curtains, and from antifreeze to toothbrushes, Dow's innovative products are essential to human progress and daily living. A leading global science and technology company, Dow and its subsidiaries have 121 manufacturing sites in 32 countries and supply customers around the globe with more than 3,500 chemical, plastic, and agricultural products.

In 1942, the Canadian government invited Dow to build a styrene plant in Sarnia, Ontario. In the following decade, the company established a presence in Alberta. Dow's manufacturing site at Fort Saskatchewan, Alberta, is now Canada's largest petrochemical complex. Set on 2,128 acres, the complex represents a $3 billion investment to date. Through the years, the Canadian sector of the company, called Dow Chemical Canada Inc., has also set up manufacturing operations in Quebec and Ontario.

Dow Chemical Canada Inc. established its headquarters in Calgary in 1996, moving from Sarnia. The move reflected a need to be closer to suppliers and an intent to focus on expanding manufacturing operations in western Canada.

"Setting up shop in Calgary means we're in the heart of the action, close to many of our peers, our customers, our competitors, and our suppliers—especially our suppliers, since we're one of the largest consumers of natural gas in the country," says Dennis Lauzon, President and CEO, Dow Chemical Canada. "Alberta has an economic environment that encourages entrepreneurship and a provincial government that supports it."

A Triple Bottom Line

Dow believes in a triple bottom line—fiscal responsibility, leadership in environmental stewardship and performance, and operations and activities that are ethically and socially responsible. That means that Dow operates as a company that is open and accountable to its communities and stakeholders, which includes issuing an annual public progress report.

Community Advisory Panels (CAPs) are another way Dow maintains relationships with the public and ensures that the company is transparent in its actions. Made up of opinion leaders, environmentalists, and industry and community members, CAPs provide opportunities for meaningful, two-way dialogue with a diverse group of residents. Dow currently has CAPs in Fort Saskatchewan, Sarnia, and Varennes, Quebec.

Dow is also committed to the principles of Responsible Care®, an initiative of the Canadian Chemical Producers' Association to improve the industry's performance and to respond to public concerns about the impact of chemicals on the environment. As part of Dow's pledge to protect the environment, and support sustainable development, the principles of Responsible Care have been threaded throughout its global operations. Throughout the life cycle of all

CLOCKWISE FROM TOP RIGHT:
AT DOW'S FORT SASKATCHEWAN SITE, CANADA GEESE ENJOY A BEAUTIFUL ALBERTA DAY ON THE COMPANY'S WILDLIFE GREENBELT, CREATED TO FOSTER NATURAL HABITAT AROUND THE SITE.

AS A MAJOR POLYSTYRENE PRODUCER, DOW IS INVOLVED WITH INITIATIVES TO COLLECT, PROCESS, AND MARKET RECYCLED POLYSTYRENE. THE POLYSTYRENE UNIT IN SARNIA PRODUCES A VERY DURABLE, HIGH-IMPACT RESIN USED IN A NUMBER OF APPLICATIONS FROM REFRIGERATOR LININGS TO BICYCLE HELMETS.

THE POWER AND UTILITIES COMBINED-CYCLE, COGENERATION PLANT AT DOW CHEMICAL CANADA INC.'S FORT SASKATCHEWAN SITE CURRENTLY GENERATES ABOUT 65 PERCENT OF THE POWER REQUIRED TO OPERATE ITS MANUFACTURING COMPLEX.

products—inception, manufacture, transportation, distribution, use, and ultimate disposal—Responsible Care guidelines and codes of practice are enforced.

Responsible Care is an ethic for operating, and is reflected in Dow's global Environment, Health & Safety Goals for the Year 2005. Targets include the reduction of waste and waste water generated per pound of production by 50 percent; decreasing motor vehicle incidents per 1 million miles by 50 percent; reducing injuries and illnesses per 200,000 work hours by 90 percent; and cutting chemical emissions by 50 percent. Internally, Dow employees call these goals the "three no's"—no accidents, no injuries, and no harm to the environment. Since announcing the goals in 1996, Dow is on course to meet and even exceed the target reductions.

Contributing to the Community

Because the support of the communities in which Dow operates is invaluable to the company's success, Dow takes pride in contributing to many local initiatives. Most of Dow's employees reside in these communities, and volunteerism and involvement are encouraged throughout the company.

As part of Dow's commitment to sustainable development, good corporate citizenship is a priority. In Calgary, Dow sponsors several programs to improve and protect the environment. For example, Dow is a sustaining partner with the Alberta Ecotrust Foundation, which works to fund numerous community environmental projects. Earth Day programs such as tree plantings are also part of Dow's dedication to the environment.

Working to foster science education, Dow provides support to the Calgary Science

PRESIDENT AND CEO OF DOW CANADA DENNIS LAUZON DIGS INTO FOREVER GREEN CALGARY, A COMMUNITY TREE-PLANTING EVENT PARTIALLY SPONSORED BY DOW.

Centre and the Calgary Science Network. The Youth Science Foundation's Canada-Wide Science Fair, as well as regional science fairs in the communities where the company operates, is a long-standing Dow endeavor.

Further Dow education projects involve a CD-ROM titled "Trading Up: Careers in Construction," to be distributed to every

high school in Alberta, aimed at increasing interest in construction trades as viable career opportunities.

A dynamic city, Calgary's economic growth and global involvement parallel Dow Chemical Canada's vision and diversity. Both the city and the company are looking forward to meeting new challenges as the new millennium unfolds.

DOW CANADA EMPLOYEES VOLUNTEER FOR A HABITAT FOR HUMANITY PROJECT, INSTALLING STYROFOAM® BRAND INSULATION DONATED BY DOW.

Engage Energy

A centre of excellence for commodity trading and energy management services, Calgary-based Engage Energy is now one of the largest Canadian-based players in the North American energy market. Offering the expertise to lead the industry and real-time market intelligence, Engage Energy provides a full spectrum of energy services, including wholesale natural gas and electricity supply aggregation and sales; natural gas and electricity trading;

energy management services; structured storage and transportation services; power management; energy risk management; and financial services.

Backed by a powerful parent company, Engage Energy has a 30-year corporate history in the North American merchant energy market. The company's parent, Westcoast Energy Inc., is a leading energy player and operates a $13 billion network of natural gas gathering, processing, transportation, storage, and distribution assets, as well as electric power generation, international, financial, information technology, and energy services businesses.

NOW ONE OF THE LARGEST CANADIAN-BASED PLAYERS IN THE NORTH AMERICAN ENERGY MARKET, ENGAGE ENERGY PROVIDES A FULL SPECTRUM OF ENERGY SERVICES, INCLUDING WHOLESALE NATURAL GAS AND ELECTRICITY SUPPLY AGGREGATION AND SALES; NATURAL GAS AND ELECTRICITY TRADING; ENERGY MANAGEMENT SERVICES; STRUCTURED STORAGE AND TRANSPORTATION SERVICES; POWER MANAGEMENT; ENERGY RISK MANAGEMENT; AND FINANCIAL SERVICES.

Energy Trading

With seven regional offices located across North America, Engage Energy operates throughout the continent. The company's some 140 employees are actively involved in most of the geographic regions where natural gas and electricity have been deregulated. Thus, Engage Energy is able to offer its clients timely information on natural gas pricing across hundreds of locations. The company's Web site at www.engageenergy.com is a valuable resource that offers up-to-date information for clients as well.

Engage Energy's pricing can be as short as one day to multiple years in duration. The company's customers can pick and choose from liquid transaction hubs to specific client locations. The firm's pricing can also include built-in flexibility and client-specific demands, allowing for custom-tailored packages.

As the electricity industry continues to evolve and change its structure, Engage Energy creates products and services to fit each market's specific characteristics, including wholesale power capacity management, as well as cross-commodity optimization for natural gas and electricity.

"We draw on a significant wealth of experience, financial strength, and integrity to deliver innovative and customized solutions to the unregulated energy market," says Mike Broadfoot, President and CEO. "Our vision is to be one of the major energy services companies in North America, providing our clients with unparalleled intellectual services."

Energy Management Services

Engage Energy provides energy management services with the goal of minimizing clients' natural gas usage, in the case of energy-consuming customers, and maximizing energy revenues

ideas to help customers rebundle their services in order to maximize the return on their energy portfolio," says Broadfoot.

Risk management is another category of services offered by Engage Energy. "We manage our own portfolio every day, so identifying risk is a skill we have finely tuned over the years," Broadfoot says. "We share this expertise so our customers can make better decisions." Through affiliates, Engage Energy also provides businesses with financial assistance for energy-related upgrades and capital investments.

A Vibrant Home for Employees

ngage Energy provides a vibrant home for people to build their careers in a fast-paced industry that rewards creativity and entrepreneurship. The expertise and knowledge of employees is crucial to the company's success, and the services provided by Engage Energy are truly intellectual capital services. "We really have no hard assets," says Broadfoot. "We depend on what's in our people's heads."

Community involvement is employee driven, but supported by the company. For example, the firm's employees are supporting a hot breakfast program for a local school; they adopt families at Christmas time; and they recently helped clean up and paint Camp Horizon, a special facility for disabled children. An employee team also taught an energy marketing course at the University of Calgary, donating their teaching earnings back to the university for student scholarships.

Engage Energy Canada's leadership in both the downtown business community and the local community at large are important contributions to the Calgary area, and will continue to play a vital role in the city's development for generations to come.

WITH SEVEN REGIONAL OFFICES LOCATED ACROSS NORTH AMERICA, ENGAGE ENERGY OPERATES THROUGHOUT THE CONTINENT.

for its energy-producing customers. In both cases, the firm is effectively able to reduce its clients' associated administrative burden. The range of services in this category include natural gas and electricity information services; supply aggregation; transmission; operations and balancing; natural gas and electricity asset management; telemetering; consolidated billing; and energy savings technology.

In addition, Engage Energy offers structured storage and transportation services. "We use innovative storage and transportation

COMMUNITY INVOLVEMENT IS EMPLOYEE DRIVEN, BUT SUPPORTED BY THE COMPANY.

Resorts of the Canadian Rockies-Skiing Louise Ltd.

esorts of the Canadian Rockies (RCR), a flourishing outdoor recreation company operated by Charlie and Louise Locke, had modest beginnings. In 1930, Sir Norman Watson—a visionary, if somewhat eccentric, Britisher—together with the renowned Swiss guides of Canadian Pacific's Chateau Lake Louise and a group of locals, formed the Ski Club of the Canadian Rockies. Their goal was to find the perfect spot to build a cabin where they could stay overnight and pursue their passion—skiing.

These early pioneers had literally millions of acres from which to choose the perfect cabin location. They finally settled on an area near Lake Louise as ideal in terms of accessibility, beauty, snow, weather, and ski terrain. Thus did Skoki, a tiny, delightful log lodge, come into being as the first multiday ski destination in western North America.

Skoki was the nucleus of what would ultimately become the Lake Louise Ski Area, now an internationally known destination resort ranking with the world's best. Likewise, Lake Louise is now the nucleus of RCR, a group of eight multisport, multiseason resorts.

RCR's resorts in the Canadian Rockies include four in Alberta—Lake Louise, Canada's favourite; Nakiska, site of the 1988 Winter Olympics; Fortress Mountain, home of freestyle skiing and snowboarding; and Wintergreen, a family facility near Calgary. In British Columbia, the company is developing destination resorts in Kimberley and Fernie, and in Quebec, four-season resorts at Mont-Sainte-Anne and Stoneham, Quebec's second- and third-largest resorts.

RESORTS OF THE CANADIAN ROCKIES (RCR), A FLOURISHING OUTDOOR RECREATION COMPANY FOUNDED BY CHARLIE AND LOUISE LOCKE, COMPRISES EIGHT RESORTS—LAKE LOUISE, NAKISKA, FORTRESS, WINTERGREEN, FERNIE ALPINE RESORT, KIMBERLY ALPINE RESORT, STONEHAM, AND MONT-SAINTE-ANNE.

The Best Vacation Possible

CR's mission is to provide its guests with the best vacation and recreational experience possible. The company's vision is to create a legacy of regional and destination resorts in Canada that set the standard for resort operations worldwide.

"Over the last 20 years, Lake Louise has invested tens of millions of dollars upgrading its facilities," says Charlie Locke, proprietor. "State-of-the-art lifts, lodges, and snow making, combined with some of the best scenery, weather, and terrain available, enable Lake Louise to compete with the best destination resorts in the world." Fernie and Kimberley are not far behind, and the company's planned investments in Quebec will ensure that the Greater Quebec City region will become the destination of choice for eastern North America.

"Lake Louise is now one of the two premier destination ski resorts in western Canada," says Locke. "It attracts more British and German skiers than any other resort in North America, and it is consistently ranked in the top 10."

A Multiseason, Multiresort, Multisport Company

hile skiing is still the major component of RCR's business, summer sports such as golf are gaining importance. The Trickle Creek Golf Course in Kimberley consistently ranks as the best golf course in British Columbia, while in Alberta and Quebec, Wintergreen and Le Grand Vallon also rank close to the top.

Some of the best sport fishing in North America is found in the Elk River at Fernie, St. Mary's River near Kimberley, and the Bow River near Wintergreen.

Most of RCR's resorts also have summer sightseeing lifts and environmental education centers. Mountain biking, hiking, horseback

THE TRICKLE CREEK RESIDENCE INN BY MARRIOTT (LEFT) AND FERNIE ALPINE RESORT OFFER EXCELLENT SKIING AND VACATION POSSIBILITIES.

LAKE LOUISE IS THE NUCLEUS OF RCR, A GROUP OF EIGHT MULTISPORT, MULTISEASON RESORTS.

riding, tennis, and casual walking are also popular activities. Whatever their passion, visitors enjoy the ample activities at all of the company's resorts during their vacation.

An Emphasis on Employees, a Passion for Excellence

hrough the company's goal of continual improvement, the customer is always assured that he will have a tremendous vacation," says Locke. "By concentrating on fixing the weakest links in the chain on a daily basis, we keep those little annoyances to a minimum. Further, all of our managers regularly take their turn at our customer service desks so as to better understand the needs of our guests."

The guests are not the only people to get the red-carpet treatment at RCR's resorts. Locke understands the benefits of having a happy staff, and provides a positive work environment by having monthly parties, offering free skiing at up to 10 areas and free golf at the company's courses, and awarding prizes for excellent service to customers. These prizes include skis, snowboards, helicopter skiing, and a chance to win free trips to Hawaii.

Locke's philosophy has earned him and his company numerous awards in past years, including Entrepreneur of the Year-Prairies Region for Tourism; one of Canada's 50 best-managed private companies; one of the 50 most influential Albertans; and awards from the Canada Ski Council and the Canada West Ski Areas Association for contributions to the industry.

"RCR has some of the best undeveloped ski-in/ski-out properties still available in North America, and at a fraction of the cost of other resorts," says Locke. "You can build your own cabin in the woods, a recreational retreat, or a retirement home at one of our resorts for much less than the cost of a lot in the United States."

Whatever the reason or the season, visitors appreciate the atmosphere of RCR ski areas because of the vacationing possibilities, the choices for entertainment, and the ability to be a part of its growing community.

KIMBERLY ALPINE RESORT (LEFT) AND CORNERSTONE LODGE IN FERNIE ARE OTHER POPULAR DESTINATIONS IN THE AREA.

Calgary Inc.

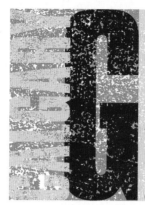

lobalization has presented Calgary with new opportunities, as well as the challenge of competing in a global marketplace while maintaining the city's quality of life, which has been recognized and acknowledged throughout the world. As the city's population speeds toward the 1 million mark, Calgarians are excited about the opportunities that this critical mass will create, yet are determined to retain the city's pioneer roots, sense of community, and entrepreneurial spirit. Calgary's approach to economic and community development will be one of balance: balance between economic prosperity and quality of life.

Calgary's rapid growth and achievement as one of Canada's most vibrant urban centres is unique. "Our pioneering heritage has given Calgary an unbeatable entrepreneurial spirit," says Mayor Al Duerr. "Calgary's rise as the nation's oil and gas hub provided us with an opportunity to grow internationally, and we are now a very cosmopolitan city with international ties in diversified industry sectors. Although Calgary competes on the global stage, we have retained our sense of community and can-do attitude that was honed so long ago. It is even more apparent and vibrant today."

Calgary is an extremely vibrant and friendly city. Located in a scenic valley where the Bow and Elbow rivers meet, Calgary's outdoor playground is truly breathtaking. Within an

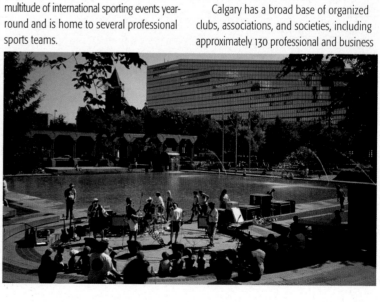

hour's drive, Calgarians can enjoy hiking, skiing, mountain biking, and a host of other activities in the majestic Rocky Mountains, Kananaskis Valley, or Banff National Park.

Enjoying leisure activities does not require leaving the city, however. Calgary boasts numerous natural park areas that are enjoyable year-round, along with one of Canada's finest pathway systems. Outdoor enthusiasts can explore approximately 300 kilometres of paved walking and cycling paths, winding through nearly 3,300 hectares of natural areas and parkland.

Numerous world-class recreational facilities, which remain as a legacy of the 1988 Olympics, can be found in Calgary. The city also hosts a multitude of international sporting events year-round and is home to several professional sports teams.

Canada's Energy Capital

As Canada's energy capital and western Canada's business capital, Calgary is now home to the second-largest concentration of corporate head offices in the nation. Due to its central location, Calgary has developed into a major distribution hub for goods and services throughout the Pacific Northwest region.

While the city's economy has been shaped primarily by the resource sector, its aggressive diversification efforts have resulted in the growth and development of both existing and emerging industry clusters in information communications technology, logistics, agrifood, the arts and culture, tourism, and wellness.

Calgary has a broad base of organized clubs, associations, and societies, including approximately 130 professional and business

organizations. These entities are representative of a large component of the technical and energy related professions, but also include organizations from almost every business sector. More than 80 trade, industry, and labor organizations meet regularly. Almost 40 percent of Calgarians are volunteers, supporting hundreds of charitable organizations located in the city. Calgary's reputation and good will, along with the generosity of its citizens, have allowed these organizations to flourish.

Hospitality and Western Spirit

As a group, Calgarians are young, highly educated, and ethnically diverse, with a pioneering intensity that has created a reputation for the city's residents as early adopters of new technology. Calgarians are also known for their warm hospitality and western spirit.

Although the city has experienced rapid growth in the past few years, Calgarians continue to cherish and protect the fundamental values that established their great city more than a century ago.

In addition, Calgarians value their environment and enviable quality of life. While enjoying their big blue sky, wide-open space, bike paths, river walks, and proximity to the mountains, citizens are extremely committed to ensuring that the city will remain a safe, compassionate place. With a strong sense of civic pride and volunteerism, Calgarians truly love to promote their city.

Celebration is an important part of life in Calgary as well. Whether hosting the world-famous Calgary Exhibition & Stampede, Spruce Meadows, World Petroleum Congress, or the upcoming 2005 Goodwill Games, Calgarians love to welcome international visitors to their community.

ALTHOUGH THE CITY HAS EXPERIENCED RAPID GROWTH IN THE PAST FEW YEARS, CALGARIANS CONTINUE TO CHERISH AND PROTECT THE FUNDAMENTAL VALUES THAT ESTABLISHED THEIR GREAT CITY MORE THAN A CENTURY AGO.

Optimism about the future characterizes Calgarians, who truly believe they can make a difference. This can-do, progressive attitude is contagious and, as a result, Calgary is extremely well positioned to be a global player in the 21st century.

Sustainable Prosperity

As the old century came to a close, the City of Calgary established Calgary Inc. to create a strategy for the future, balancing economic prosperity and quality of life. Calgary Inc. defines this unique balance as sustainable prosperity.

"Sustainable prosperity is an innovative and bold notion," says Georgine Ulmer, President and CEO of Calgary Inc. "It's built on the ideals of community, integrity, business, safe, clean, progressive, fun, and western. It fosters leadership and citizen engagement, and expects a return on community values. If Calgary truly is to be a city that lives our values, Calgary's Community Strategy for Sustainable Prosperity will help ensure that all of our activities are in fact contributing towards achieving our vision."

Sustainable prosperity will change the way Calgarians develop, implement, and evaluate their community and economic development activities. Calgary Inc.'s Community Strategy for Sustainable Prosperity will not only secure Calgary's position as a desirable city in which to live and do business, but also connect Calgarians to each other and to the world. Calgary's residents are excited about shaping their future. The city's new slogan says it all: Calgary, Heart of the New West.

Sanmina Canada ULC

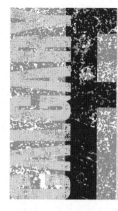

ounded in 1980 as a manufacturer of printed circuit boards, Sanmina Canada ULC's growing expertise led the company to produce more sophisticated backplane assemblies and subassemblies by the late 1980s. Following this successful building block strategy, Sanmina entered the contract manufacturing industry in 1994. ❧ With a worldwide employee base at greater than 20,000, Sanmina is one of the most successful and fastest-growing providers of turnkey electron-

ics manufacturing services (EMS) in the world. The company is one of only a few to meet the high-tech industry's demand for single-source contract manufacturing and assembly services. Specific target markets are the telecommunications and data communications, medical, and high-end computing industries.

With head offices in San Jose, the company is expanding rapidly to meet the needs of a diverse customer base. There are more than 50 manufacturing facilities configured to serve the high-growth segments of the global, US$95 billion EMS industry.

A key to the company's success is its vertical integration—its ability to call on a number of company-owned entities for a variety of components and services. This one-stop manufacturing solution is a key competitive advantage that gives Sanmina greater control over quality, delivery, time to market, and cost—to the benefit of its customers. Sanmina's engineers work with customer design teams early in the development cycle, making it easier and more cost effective to implement changes prior to full production. Customers who rely on the company as their single-source supplier reduce their overall manufacturing costs, as well as improving their product designs

and the speed with which they introduce new products to the marketplace.

Calgary Operation

One of Sanmina's first presences in Canada was its Calgary Systems Manufacturing operation, established in 1999. "Nortel was planning to divest some of its manufacturing opera-

tions that were not considered part of the company's core competencies," says Mike Shannon, a former Nortel employee and now Senior Vice-President of EMS Operations, Canada, for Sanmina. "Nortel had a 20-year relationship with Sanmina, and so it was decided that Sanmina would start up a local operation supplying Nortel."

There were 110 highly trained employees

SANMINA CANADA ULC'S CALGARY FACILITY PLAYS A KEY ROLE IN THE COMPANY'S OVERALL STRATEGY, AS IT ESTABLISHES ITSELF AS THE RADIO FREQUENCY (WIRELESS) CENTRE OF EXCELLENCE SERVING THE TELECOMMUNICATION, MICROWAVE, AND FIXED WIRELESS INDUSTRIES.

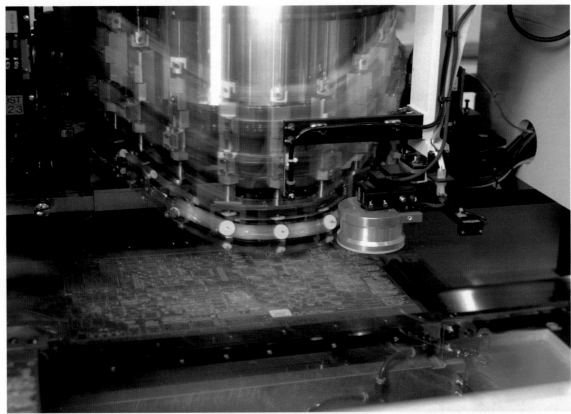

who made the transfer from Nortel Networks to Sanmina, which was accomplished in a single day—dismantling equipment on a Friday and reassembling it the following day in a new location. Production was only down for 25 hours altogether. "I think that's spectacular," says Shannon. "That's the Calgary can-do attitude."

Sanmina knew the Calgary location would have a number of benefits in addition to the enthusiasm for which Calgarians are so well known. Besides being close to a number of high-tech customers, Calgary offers access to a highly trained labor pool from the Southern and Northern Alberta Institutes of Technology (SAIT and NAIT), as well the University of Calgary. If the company should need to look beyond Alberta's borders, Calgary offers a lifestyle for potential employees that is second to none.

Key Role in Strategy

The Calgary facility plays a key role in Sanmina's overall strategy, as it establishes itself as the radio frequency (wireless) centre of excellence serving the telecommunication, microwave, and fixed wireless industries.

The company has more than 90,000 square feet of manufacturing space in two plants, as well as office and laboratory space nearby. With the recent addition of a design team and product integrity testing facility, the Calgary operation provides full turnkey electronics manufacturing—from conception to design, prototype development, production ramp-up, and regulatory testing and compliance. The product testing facility is state of the art and is replicated in very few places throughout the world.

Growing Fast

Hiring is ongoing for Sanmina's Calgary operation, which employs more than 800 people. Shannon sits on an industrial advisory board for SAIT, providing input on the types of employees needed for the industry and the type of training they require. "We're also working with Bow Valley College to develop customized training programs, which is a true win-win situation for our organizations," Shannon says.

Shannon is also chairman of the Strategic Planning Committee for the Calgary Science Centre. "We see a need to educate the younger crowd—kids ages five to 10—about the technology fundamental, and the science centre provides us with many opportunities

to do so," says Shannon.

Clearly, the Calgary operation has been given a good deal of autonomy to accomplish its objectives. "We never say no to a customer," says Shannon. "We'll always find a way to make it work. That's the Sanmina difference."

Sanmina's unique capabilities provide cost-effective solutions that meet the needs of enterprises at the forefront of the high-tech industry. Sanmina will continue to strengthen its position as a global pioneer through strategic acquisitions and investments in state-of-the-art facilities. The company's full spectrum of integrated service capabilities, diverse customer base, and worldwide reach will ensure its success as a leader in the future of electronics manufacturing and associated services. And the Calgary operation will continue to play a key role in helping Sanmina Canada ULC achieve its goals.

Corus Radio Calgary

he name may be new, but Corus Radio Calgary has been providing radio news, music, and entertainment for as long as most Calgarians can remember. Corus' three radio stations—Country 105, POWER 107, and CHQR AM 770—dominate the radio industry in southern Alberta. Each is number one in the market it services, with a combined reach of more than 500,000 listeners each week. ❖ "No other radio group has such strength across these markets,"

says Corus Radio Calgary General Manager Rick Meaney. "All three of our stations are exciting and dynamic, reflecting the city where we're located. As Calgary continues to grow, so will we."

The stations are as responsive to advertisers as they are to listeners, collaborating with the business community to produce award-winning radio commercials. The Corus trio offers advertisers a balanced quality audience, delivering both males and females in all key buying demographics. Almost 75 percent of the three stations'

audiences fall into the 18-to-54 age group of consumers, making the stations very attractive to advertisers.

Changing the Face of Entertainment

Corus Radio Calgary is a division of Corus Entertainment Inc., one of Canada's leading media companies. Its principal assets consist of 49 radio stations, specialty television networks, Pay TV, and conventional television assets. Corus is also prominent in the digital music market and various advertising services companies.

A publicly traded company, Corus is listed on the Toronto Stock Exchange (CJR.B) and the New York Stock Exchange (CJR).

Created from the media assets of Shaw Communications Inc., Corus Entertainment is a dynamic collection of trail-blazing properties that will continue to change the face of entertainment. The company is committed to delivering superior results, adding value with an aggressive acquisition program.

Corus Entertainment has evolved from a vision to create a strong, vertically integrated Canadian media company, capable of competing against dominant global players. With a focus on children's entertainment and music, the company's mandate will continue to include a strong commitment to Canadian programming and talent. For example, Corus broadcast the 10th anniversary YTV Youth Achievement Awards and cosponsored the Canadian Country Music Awards.

Country 105

One of Calgary's most honoured radio stations is Corus-owned Country 105 (CKRY-FM). Country 105 focuses on playing Today's Best Country—featuring artists such as Calgary's own Paul Brandt, the Dixie Chicks, Shania Twain, George Strait, Tim McGraw, Alan Jackson, Faith Hill, the Wilkinsons, Reba McEntire, and Garth Brooks. The station's target demographic group is 25- to 54-year-olds.

Country 105 first went on the air on July 9, 1982, and the first song played was "Are You Ready for the Country?" by Waylon Jennings. In 1993, the station moved its studios from 14th Street NW to Centre Street. In 1997, the ownership of the station transferred from Redmond Broadcasting to Shaw Radio, and the studios moved into Shaw Court in downtown Calgary in 1998. In 1999, Country 105 became part of the Corus Entertainment family.

Country 105 has been named Station of the Year every year since 1993 by the Canadian Country Music Association, and has earned the On-Air Personality of the Year award in that same span. The station's Phil Kallsen has been honoured a number of times as Music Director of the Year. Country 105 was also the recipient of *RPM* magazine's

COUNTRY 105 (CKRY-FM), OWNED BY CORUS RADIO CALGARY, FOCUSES ON PLAYING TODAY'S BEST COUNTRY. IT HAS BEEN NAMED STATION OF THE YEAR EVERY YEAR SINCE 1993 BY THE CANADIAN COUNTRY MUSIC ASSOCIATION.

Big Country Award honouring distinguished achievement in the Canadian country music industry in 1995 and 1996.

Country 105 was also the only Canadian country radio station to be nominated in both 1999 and 2000 by the U.S. Country Music Association for its annual awards held in Nashville. The station has also received awards from both the Canadian and the Western Association of Broadcasters, and has won numerous awards for its advertising commercials as well. In 1999, the station was an Ad Rodeo winner for its Imax Knife Edge, and received an Ad Rodeo Certificate of Merit for its Family Values commercial.

That year the station was also a New York Festival finalist for its "High Cost of Smoking" and "The Ins and Outs of Smoking" public service announcements.

The station's mission is stated as follows: "Each day we will strive to connect with the community through compelling entertainment. With a strong commitment to integrity and excellence, we will consistently relate to our listeners by delivering passion and originality."

Country 105 broadcasts at an authorized power of 100,000 watts and at a frequency of 105.1 MHz. The station can also be heard at 96.3 on local cable TV. Its broadcast foot-print extends north of Innisfail, east of Bassano, south of Claresholm, and west towards Banff. Country 105 also broadcasts to the community of Banff on its own repeater. Computer users can listen to the station on the World Wide Web at country 105.com, while TV viewers can hear the station on the Bell ExpressVu Satellite Channel 975.

POWER 107

Another crown jewel for Corus is POWER 107 (CKIK-FM), a fun, entertaining, hip station that appeals to Calgarians who want to listen to current hits. POWER 107 plays Today's Best

Music in a top 40 format that launched at 1:07 p.m., Friday, September 26, 1997. Since the new format launch, POWER 107 has seen explosive growth in all demographic groups to the point where the station is now a top runner in the city.

With more than 300,000 weekly listeners, POWER 107 is the perfect match for Calgary's dynamic young population. Like Country 105, POWER 107 is sensitive to its audience and endeavours to play the music they want to hear, with artists like Ricky Martin, Backstreet Boys, Madonna, the Moffatts, U2, Matchbox Twenty, Barenaked Ladies, and Janet Jackson.

POWER 107 has become the first choice for record companies, concert promoters, and movie distributors to introduce their newest releases. POWER 107 is also the choice of nightclubs and restaurants—the station is live on location in clubs around town, six nights a week.

A mainstay of the station has been its flagship promotion, the Phrase That Pays. The phrase's 11 words—POWER 107 Plays Today's Best Music, Now Show Me My Money!—have rewarded Calgarians to the tune of hundreds of thousands of dollars in cash and prizes since the promotion kicked off with the station launch in the fall of 1997.

POWER has won the *Calgary Herald* Readers Choice as Calgary's most popular radio station for three years running, and has won similar awards from publications such as *Fast Forward* and *Calgary Child.*

ON THE AIR DURING THE MID-DAY SHIFT AT POWER 107 (CKIK-FM), LISTENERS TUNE IN TO HEAR THEIR FAVORITE TOP 40 HITS. ON-LINE, THEY CAN LISTEN TO THE STATION AT WWW.POWER107.COM

POWER has also been nominated as CHR (contemporary hits radio) Station of the Year for three years in a row.

POWER 107 broadcasts at an authorized power of 100,000 watts at a frequency of 107.3 MHz (98.7 on FM cable). Its broadcast footprint extends north beyond Red Deer, east beyond Drumheller, and south to Claresholm. POWER 107 also has a repeater in the resort townsite of Banff in the Rocky Mountains west of Calgary. On-line listeners can listen to the station at its Web site, www.power107.com.

CHQR AM 770

CHQR AM 770 offers listeners a dedicated news and talk show format. CHQR AM 770 is Calgary News/Talk/Sports, providing a comprehensive news package, while the talk element gives listeners an opportunity to talk about the news they have just heard. CHQR is also streaming audio on the Internet at www.qr77.com.

Since launching the news and talk format in 1994, the station has enjoyed steady

MOST OF THE COMMERCIALS, SPLITTERS, AND PROMOTIONAL ANNOUNCEMENTS FOR POWER 107 AND CHQR ARE PRODUCED IN ONE OF THE IN-HOUSE STUDIOS.

growth. Reaching an adult and affluent audience ages 35 to 54, CHQR is far and away the most listened to AM station in the city, and Calgary's first choice for radio news, traffic, weather, sports, and business information. Extremely responsive, CHQR will break its programming to provide critical news to listeners.

CHQR's Dave Rutherford is one of the most respected talk show hosts in Canada, and the only national daily syndicated talk show host in private radio. He is a broadcast veteran, having spent more than a quarter of a century in the business. Rutherford has been a newsman, a news director, and a program director, but now spends his time preparing and hosting his daily talk show. He is also one of the founding directors of CHQR's special charity, the Calgary Children's Foundation (CCF).

CCF is a fundraising partnership with the Westin Hotel in Calgary, and raises money to support children in need. The highpoint of each year's fundraising efforts is the annual pledge day on CHQR, which regularly raises in excess of $125,000.

CHQR also airs a morning show with Bruce Kenyon, "Open Line" afternoons with Dave Taylor, "Calgary Today" with Dave Arnold, and "Sportstalk" with Mark Stephen—a nightly, two-hour, open-line sports show that is the only one of its kind in Calgary.

CHQR is the broadcast rights holder for the Calgary Stampeders Football Club. The Stampeders are the flagship franchise in the CFL, regularly drawing record audiences both at the stadium and on the radio.

Community Involvement

All three stations are extremely active in the community, each choosing charitable and community causes in keeping with the demographics of its listeners. Helping others is a year-round activity for the stations. At any given point in time, there is always at least one cause being supported. Among them are the Calgary Children's Foundation, Mustard Seed Ministry, Calgary Inter-faith Food Bank, United Way, Calgary Humane Society, Salvation Army, and a Christmas toy drive, to name only a few.

Corus Radio Calgary reaches Calgarians—whether they are waking up, driving to work, or listening on the Internet—and its three radio stations play a key role in making the city such a dynamic and thriving community.

POWER 107 IS THE NUMBER ONE HIT RADIO STATION IN CALGARY, AND HAS SEEN EXPLOSIVE GROWTH IN ALL DEMOGRAPHIC GROUPS.

THE ANNOUNCERS THAT ANIMATE CHQR'S PROGRAMMING ARE BRUCE KENYON ("MORNING SHOW"), DAVE TAYLOR ("QR77 AFTERNOONS"), AND DAVE ARNOLD ("CALGARY TODAY").

UtiliCorp Networks Canada

Deregulation of the electric industry in Alberta has opened the door to competition and new companies, with the ultimate goal of providing a choice of suppliers and competitive prices for energy consumers. One of the province's newest players is UtiliCorp Networks Canada. In 2000, the company purchased TransAlta Corporation's southern Alberta-based electricity distribution and retail operations for C$645 million, and subsequently reached an agreement with EPCOR for that company to provide UtiliCorp's 350,000 customers with retail power and related services. The move allows Calgary-based UtiliCorp Networks Canada to focus on the safe, reliable operation of the 90,000 kilometres of low-voltage power distribution lines that serve those Alberta customers.

Public Utility Roots

Based in Kansas City, Missouri, UtiliCorp United is an international energy and services company that was formed in 1985 from Missouri Public Service Company. The company has created a strong presence in the United States as a provider of competitive and innovative energy solutions, and has a growing presence in the international arena. UtiliCorp serves about 4 million customers across the United States and in Canada, the United Kingdom, New Zealand, and Australia.

Led by its Aquila Energy unit, which also operates from offices in Calgary as Aquila Canada, UtiliCorp in 1999 was ranked the second-largest wholesale marketer of electricity in North America, as well as the third-largest marketer of natural gas. At June 30, 2000, the company's assets were C$13 billion, with annual sales of C$31.6 billion. UtiliCorp was also ranked 90th on *Fortune* magazine's Fortune 500 list, and is included on Fortune's list of America's Most Admired Companies.

UtiliCorp's first international foray was the purchase of West Kootenay Power in British Columbia in 1987. Throughout the 1990s, the company increased its holdings in the United States and made energy investments in New Zealand and Australia. By the end of the decade, the energy market in Alberta was providing an inviting climate for new players, and UtiliCorp was one of the first to recognize the opportunity.

An Ideal Fit

One of our plans for growth calls for expanding our operations into deregulating energy markets that are based on strong economies," says Robert Holzwarth, CEO of UtiliCorp Networks Canada. "Alberta represents an ideal fit with that strategy."

The safe, efficient management of energy networks around the world is one of UtiliCorp's principal strengths. The company is committed to establishing a strong local presence in Alberta; the firm's headquarters in Calgary is guided by a team comprised of personnel from TransAlta, from the West Kootenay subsidiary, and from elsewhere in the company's global operations.

"Decisions will be made on the ground in Alberta," explains Holzwarth. "While we closely coordinate our activities with UtiliCorp's corporate staff in Kansas City, the business model we follow allows each of our units to be run nearly autonomously, with maximum flexibility to respond to the local needs and expectations in the service area."

Synergies with Alberta

While UtiliCorp may be a new player in Alberta, in many ways the company feels right at home. The Alberta market is very similar to UtiliCorp's

BOB HOLZWORTH IS CURRENT PRESIDENT AND CEO OF UTILICORP NETWORKS CANADA (LEFT).

THE COMPANY'S SLOGAN—SMART. SIMPLE. ENERGY.— HELPS KEEP EMPLOYEES FOCUSED ON PROVIDING ENERGY SOLUTIONS TO CUSTOMERS AROUND THE GLOBE (RIGHT).

operations in Kansas and Missouri—a balanced mix of industrial, commercial, and residential customers in rural and urban settings. Both Calgary and Kansas City are medium-sized metropolitan areas with strong, modern economies built on colorful traditions in the development of the western part of North America.

Both cities are big enough to offer residents and visitors a rich menu of activities in the arts, cultural variety, and professional sports, yet both are small enough to maintain a healthy focus on community and neighborhoods. "Calgary has its annual Stampede," says Holzwarth, "while Kansas City presents the American Royal each fall involving rodeo, horse, and cattle shows and competitions; barbecue cooking; and music performances."

UtiliCorp managers have worked diligently to assure the change-over with TransAlta was done right—in other words, totally uneventfully for customers. UtiliCorp's role as a corporate citizen is still being determined, but local community participation will likely be similar to TransAlta's involvement over the years.

The company also plans to introduce its sophisticated customer information system to its Alberta operations. "The system is one of the best in the industry, and helps us provide excellent service in a cost-effective manner," says Holzwarth.

As for the future, UtiliCorp intends to grow further in Canada. Coupled with West Kootenay Power in British Columbia, the new Alberta operations will provide a strong foundation for pursuing energy assets, alliances, and partnerships in other provinces. The company's slogan—Smart. Simple. Energy.—

helps keep employees focused on providing energy solutions to customers around the globe.

"Our strongest commitment is to quality customer service," says Holzwarth. "To meet that commitment, we can draw on a broad range of experience—from Missouri to Melbourne, from Colorado to the European continent. We're essentially small-town people who've learned how to serve diverse markets and cultures around the world. Our people have a long history of believing in themselves and their company."

UtiliCorp obviously understands what Calgary is all about—and will have no trouble at all fitting right in.

SAVED FROM THE WRECKING BALL BY THE COMPANY'S DECISION TO INVEST MORE THAN US$30 MILLION IN ITS RESTORATION, UTILICORP UNITED'S WORLD HEADQUARTERS OCCUPIES A 112-YEAR-OLD, HISTORIC BUILDING IN DOWNTOWN KANSAS CITY, MISSOURI.

THE COMPANY'S LEADERSHIP CONSISTS OF (SEATED, FROM LEFT) ROBERT HOBBS, V.P., REGULATORY AND LEGISLATIVE SERVICES; LYN BROWN, V.P. OF CORPORATE COMMUNICATIONS; AND CHUCK LEE, V.P. OF BUSINESS PLANNING & PERFORMANCE MANAGEMENT (STANDING, FROM LEFT) DON DEBIENNE, V.P. OF NETWORK OPERATIONS; BOB HOLZWARTH, PRESIDENT AND CEO; RICH KRAMER, V.P. OF ADMINISTRATION; FAUZIA LALANI, V.P. OF CUSTOMER CARE; PEARSE WALSH, WHO IS NOW WITH UTILICORP COMMUNICATIONS SERVICES; AND BILL VAN YZERLOO, CHIEF FINANCIAL OFFICER.

JORO Manufacturing Company Ltd.

The science of ergonomics, which deals with the ideal proportions of the human figure, has been around for a number of centuries. Ergonomics in the office, hitherto reserved for office chairs and keyboard trays, provided an improvement in the working conditions but fell short of the complete solution. One of the missing components, the height adjustable work station, has been around for many years but only started to gain acceptance in the mid-1990s. As a result, what was once considered a novelty item is now becoming an integral part of the office environment.

Headquartered in Airdrie with new manufacturing facilities, JORO Manufacturing Company Ltd. began operations in 1996 with unique and carefully thought-out designs.

After many years of extensive research and development, JORO now produces three major lines of height adjustable furniture and accessories. All take advantage of a unique and proprietary height adjustment mechanism that ensures smooth and repeatable operation.

The LC Series, JORO's flagship line, supports the vast needs of the corporate world. This series carries many standard sizes, yet it offers an enormous degree of flexibility and customization. This has resulted in breakthrough designs for clients, including retrofit models that attach to existing office panels.

JORO also offers a home office version of its corporate furniture line. This modular series

is standardized and designed to fit the spaces of home offices. Through product standardization, this series can be offered at a modest rate even with its high-end features.

In addition to office furniture, JORO also caters to the children's market. The GroDESK series is suitable for children aged four to early teens, and is durable, easy to maintain, and intended for use both at home and in school. GroDESK allows children to sit or stand at their desk, as well as ensuring that they have a properly fitted desk as they continue to grow.

Unmatched Customization

"One of our main strengths is our ability to customize our work stations," says Shary Anton, Vice-President, marketing. "We can create any desk shape requested by clients and we do it cost effectively. JORO's system is engineered to allow components to be 'stretched and pulled' to accommodate any design or space requirements quickly within standard delivery times and with little or no increase in price."

In addition, JORO's work station tops are wrapped with a seamless thermofoil so that, with the aid of computer software and computer-navigated machinery, any top shape is possible. "We've created every top shape from the traditional right angles to the free-form organic shapes void of hard edges," says Anton. "This system allows incredible design possibilities."

JORO is able to offer all of its high-quality products at very reasonable prices due to efficient manufacturing processes and product assembly. Delivery times are generally short, taking an average of three to four weeks from the time of the initial purchase order.

Because Calgary is a corporate city with the second-largest number of head offices in Canada and with many international connections, the city provides a favourable environment for the high-end office furniture business. It's an industry that is expected to continue to grow rapidly.

"Our product and philosophy have led us into the international arena, and we look to further our position with new concepts and designs," says Anton. "We have already established a very strong presence in the market, and we are very excited about our developments for the upcoming years."

JORO MANUFACTURING COMPANY LTD. BEGAN OPERATIONS IN 1996 WITH UNIQUE AND CAREFULLY THOUGHT-OUT DESIGNS. JORO IS ABLE TO OFFER ALL OF ITS HIGH-QUALITY PRODUCTS AT VERY REASONABLE PRICES DUE TO EFFICIENT MANUFACTURING PROCESSES AND PRODUCT ASSEMBLY.

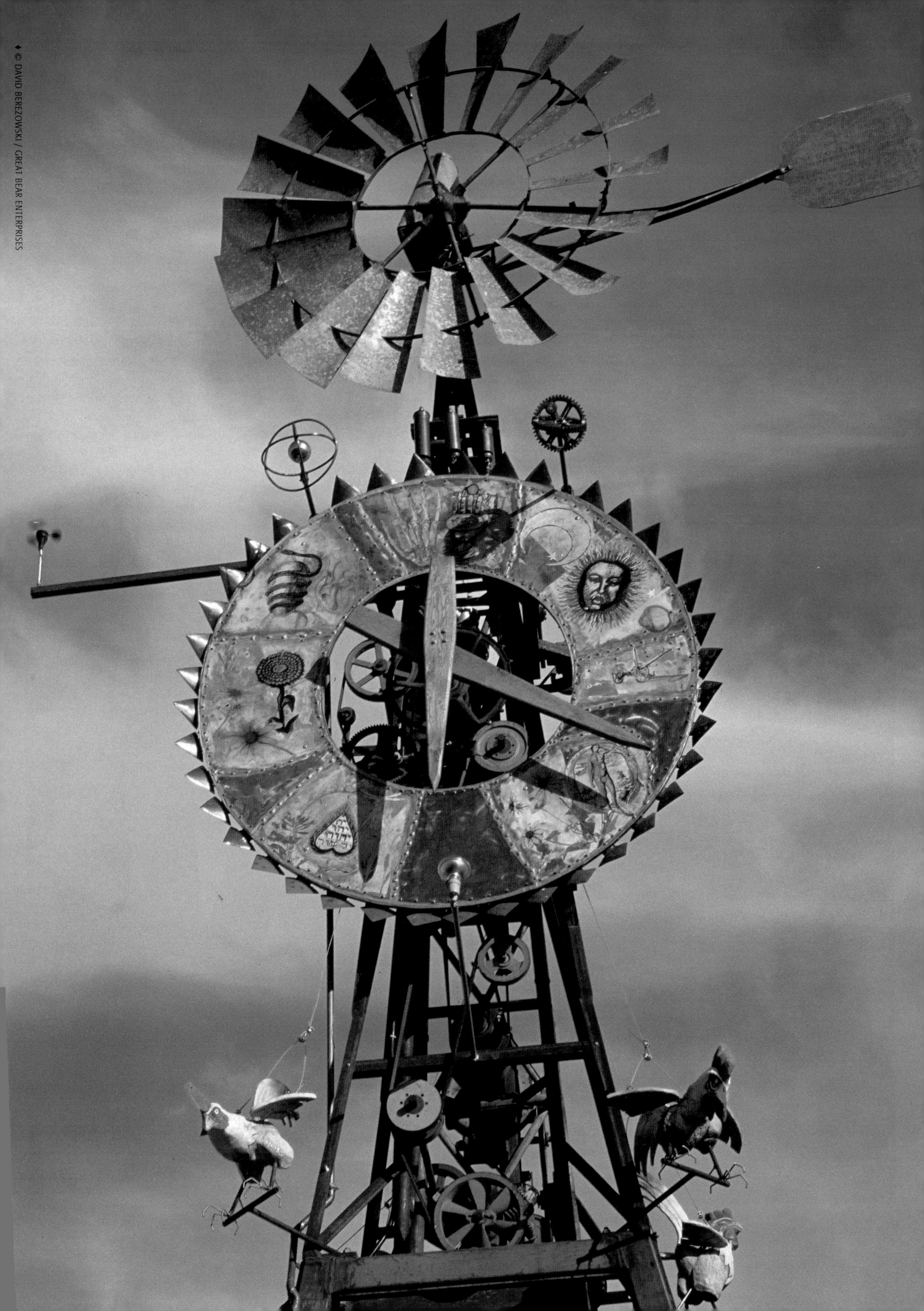

Towery Publishing, Inc.

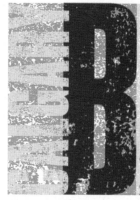

Beginning as a small publisher of local newspapers in the 1930s, Towery Publishing, Inc. today produces a wide range of community-oriented materials, including books (Urban Tapestry Series), business directories, magazines, and Internet publications. Building on its long heritage of excellence, the company has become global in scope, with cities from San Diego to Sydney represented by Towery products. In all its endeavors,

this Memphis-based company strives to be synonymous with service, utility, and quality. Over the years, Towery has become the largest producer of published materials for North American chambers of commerce. From membership directories that enhance business-to-business communication to visitor and relocation guides tailored to reflect the unique qualities of the communities they cover, the company's chamber-oriented materials offer comprehensive information on dozens of topics, including housing, education, leisure activities, health care, and local government.

In 1998, the company acquired Cincinnati-based Target Marketing, an established pro-

vider of detailed city street maps to more than 200 chambers of commerce throughout the United States and Canada. Now a division of Towery, Target offers full-color maps that include local landmarks and points of interest, such as recreational parks, shopping centers, golf courses, schools, industrial parks, city and county limits, subdivision names, public buildings, and even block numbers on most streets.

In 1990, Towery launched the Urban Tapestry Series, an award-winning collection of oversized, hardbound photojournals detailing the people, history, culture, environment, and commerce of various metropolitan areas. These coffee-table books highlight a com-

munity through three basic elements: an introductory essay by a noted local individual, an exquisite collection of four-color photographs, and profiles of the companies and organizations that animate the area's business life.

To date, more than 80 Urban Tapestry Series editions have been published in cities around the world, from New York to Vancouver to Sydney. Authors of the books' introductory essays include former U.S. President Gerald Ford (Grand Rapids), CFCN's long-time news anchor Darrell Janz (Calgary), CBS anchor Dan Rather (Austin), ABC anchor Hugh Downs (Phoenix), best-selling mystery author Robert B. Parker

THE TOWERY FAMILY'S PUBLISHING ROOTS CAN BE TRACED TO 1935, WHEN R.W. TOWERY (FAR LEFT) BEGAN PRODUCING A SERIES OF COMMUNITY HISTORIES IN TENNESSEE, MISSISSIPPI, AND TEXAS. THROUGHOUT THE COMPANY'S HISTORY, THE FOUNDING FAMILY HAS CONSISTENTLY EXHIBITED A COMMITMENT TO CLARITY, PRECISION, INNOVATION, AND VISION.

(Boston), American Movie Classics host Nick Clooney (Cincinnati), Senator Richard Lugar (Indianapolis), and Challenger Center founder June Scobee Rodgers (Chattanooga).

To maintain hands-on quality in all of its periodicals and books, Towery has long used the latest production methods available. The company was the first production environment in the United States to combine desktop publishing with color separations and image scanning to produce finished film suitable for burning plates for four-color printing. Today, Towery relies on state-of-the-art digital prepress services to produce more than 8,000 pages each year, containing well over 30,000 high-quality color images.

An Internet Pioneer

By combining its long-standing expertise in community-oriented published materials with advanced sales force, and extensive data management capabilities, Towery has emerged as a significant provider of Internet-based city information. In keeping with its overall focus on community resources, the company's Internet efforts represent a natural step in the evolution of the business.

The primary product lines within the Internet division are the introCity™ sites. Towery's introCity sites introduce newcomers, visitors, and longtime residents to every facet of a particular community, while simultaneously placing the local chamber of commerce at the forefront of the city's Internet activity. The sites include newcomer information, calendars, photos, citywide business listings with everything from nightlife to shopping to family fun, and on-line maps pinpointing the exact

location of businesses, schools, attractions, and much more.

Decades of Publishing Expertise

In 1972, current President and CEO J. Robert Towery succeeded his parents in managing the printing and publishing business they had founded nearly four decades earlier. Soon thereafter, he expanded the scope of the company's published materials to include *Memphis* magazine and other successful regional and national publications. In 1985, after selling its locally focused assets, Towery began the trajectory on which it continues today, creating community-oriented materials that are often produced in conjunction with chambers of commerce and other business organizations.

Despite the decades of change, Towery himself follows a long-standing family philosophy of unmatched service and unflinching quality. That approach extends throughout the entire organization to include more than 120 employees at the Memphis headquarters, another 80 located in Northern Kentucky outside Cincinnati, and more than 40 sales, marketing, and editorial staff traveling to and working in a growing list of client cities. All of its products, and more information about the company, are featured on the Internet at www.towery.com.

In summing up his company's steady growth, Towery restates the essential formula that has driven the business since its first pages were published: "The creative energies of our staff drive us toward innovation and invention. Our people make the highest possible demands on themselves, so I know that our future is secure if the ingredients for success remain a focus on service and quality."

TOWERY PUBLISHING PRESIDENT AND CEO J. ROBERT TOWERY HAS EXPANDED THE BUSINESS HIS PARENTS STARTED IN THE 1930S TO INCLUDE A GROWING ARRAY OF TRADITIONAL AND ELECTRONIC PUBLISHED MATERIALS, AS WELL AS INTERNET AND MULTIMEDIA SERVICES, THAT ARE MARKETED LOCALLY, NATIONALLY, AND INTERNATIONALLY.

TOWERY PUBLISHING WAS THE FIRST PRODUCTION ENVIRONMENT IN THE UNITED STATES TO COMBINE DESKTOP PUBLISHING WITH COLOR SEPARATIONS AND IMAGE SCANNING TO PRODUCE FINISHED FILM SUITABLE FOR BURNING PLATES FOR FOUR-COLOR PRINTING. TODAY, THE COMPANY'S STATE-OF-THE-ART NETWORK OF MACINTOSH AND WINDOWS WORKSTATIONS ALLOWS IT TO PRODUCE MORE THAN 8,000 PAGES EACH YEAR, CONTAINING MORE THAN 30,000 HIGH-QUALITY COLOR IMAGES.

Photographers

Originally headquartered in London, ALLSPORT has expanded to include offices in New York and Los Angeles. Its pictures have appeared in every major publication in the world, and the best of its portfolio has been displayed at elite photographic exhibitions at the Royal Photographic Society and the Olympic Museum in Lausanne.

Co-owner of Great Bear Enterprises, DAVID BEREZOWSKI specializes in photojournalism and landscape photography, and his clients include Gem Trek Publishing and the Calgary Convention and Visitors Bureau. In 1986 and 1987, he won Kodak Canada awards for the best sports photograph published in a Saskatchewan community newspaper.

A digital imaging technician at the University of Calgary, JAMES BURTON works as a professional freelance photographer, as well as a stock photographer for the Mach 2 Stock Exchange Ltd.

JAN BUTCHOFSKY-HOUSER specializes in travel photography and has co-authored the third edition of a travel guidebook, *Hidden Mexico*. Her photos have appeared in dozens of magazines, newspapers, books, advertisements, and brochures, as well as on video and album covers. She has served as an editorial/research associate for the Berkeley, California-based Ulysses Press and currently manages Dave G. Houser Stock Photography. Her honors include two Bronze awards from the Society of American Travel Writers.

CRAIG DOUCE specializes in industry photography, newspaper photojournalism, and portraiture, as well as skateboarding, snowboarding, and BMX images. His photographs have appeared in the Walter Phillips Gallery in Banff and in the Bellevue Art Museum in Bellevue, Washington.

After moving to Calgary in 1994, SHANNON WELLS DUNCAN worked in the photo department and later as a staff photographer at *The Calgary Herald.* She specializes in equine photography and served as a photographer on the set of *Jet Boy*, a 2001 motion picture release.

LEE FOSTER, a veteran travel writer and photographer, has had his work published in major travel magazines and newspapers. He maintains a stock library that features images of more than 250 destinations around the world.

Originally from Calgary, LEAH HENNEL works for *The Calgary Sun* and specializes in photojournalism. Her images have been published in *Western Horseman* magazine.

A contributing editor to *Vacations and Cruises & Tours* magazines, and co-author of the travel guidebook *Hidden Coast of California*, DAVE G. HOUSER specializes in cruise/luxury travel, personality, health, and history photography. He has been a runner-up for the Lowell Thomas Travel Journalist of the Year Award and was named the 1984 Society of American Travel Writers' Photographer of the Year.

Specializing in photography and large-scale computer imaging, KEVIN JORDAN has images in permanent collections at the Canadian National Archives, the Alberta Foundation for the Arts, and the Museum of Contemporary Photography. He has received awards from such organizations as the Alberta Professional Photographers Association, the American Professional Photographers Association, and the Alberta Foundation for the Arts.

Specializing in outdoor, nature, corporate, and agricultural photography, JERRY KAUTZ owns Kautz Photography & Graphic Design, and has had countless images in promotional materials for national and international clients. He recently embarked on a six-week, 15,000-kilometre photo assignment to Manitoba to photograph wildlife for Heartland Associates' *Pelicans to Polar Bears: Watching Wildlife in Manitoba.*

Based in Austin, Texas, location photographer ED LALLO creates high-impact commercial and editorial images for advertising and public relations agencies, design studios, corporations, and news and feature media. His work appears in brochures for AT&T, Hallmark Cards, and Sheraton Hotels, and his clients include *People, Ladies' Home Journal,* and *McCall's.*

Working for worldwide agencies and corporations such as the Mach 2 Stock Exchange Ltd., TRUDIE LEE has established a strong foothold in arts

and entertainment, and specializes in high-profile assignments that include food, product, and architecture photography.

A native of Whitehorse, Yukon, LARRY MACDOUGAL has lived in and photographed Canadian cities as far-flung as Halifax and Vancouver. He specializes in editorial and stock photography, and his images have been used by companies based in Calgary, Edmonton, and Ottawa. His work has garnered three Canadian National Newspaper and two Canadian Press Picture of the Year awards in news and sports photography.

THE MACH 2 STOCK EXCHANGE LTD. is owned and operated by Pamela Varga. Founded in Calgary in 1986, the company represents 60 photographers across Canada and the United States, and has business affiliates in New York, Paris, London, Hong Kong, Beijing, and Shanghai. Its images have been sold to such major companies as the Ford Motor Company in Detroit, the Bank of Asia, Canon Digital Cameras, and Panasonic.

Specializing in lifestyle and industrial photography, BILL MARSH owns Bill Marsh Photography and contributes to the Mach 2 Stock Exchange Ltd.